Due Process Denied: Detentions and Deportations in the United States

Tanya Golash-Boza

Due process protections are among the most important constitutional protections in the United States, yet they do not apply to non-citizens facing detention and deportation. *Due Process Denied* describes the consequences of this lack of due process through the stories of deportees and detainees. People who have lived nearly all of their lives in the United States have been detained and deported for minor crimes, without regard for constitutional limits on disproportionate punishment. The court's insistence that deportation is not punishment does not align with the experiences of deportees. For many, deportation is one of the worst imaginable punishments.

Tanya Golash-Boza is an Assistant Professor of Sociology and American Studies at the University of Kansas. She is the author of two books: *Yo Soy Negro: Blackness in Peru* (University Press of Florida, 2011) and *Immigration Nation: Raids, Detentions and Deportations in Post-9/11 America* (Paradigm Publishers, 2012), as well as dozens of peer-reviewed articles, book chapters, and essays in online and print magazines.

D1569768

WITHDRAWN

 **University Readers** Reading Materials Evolved.

THE SOCIAL ISSUES COLLECTION™

 **Routledge** Taylor & Francis Group

Framing 21st Century Social Issues

The goal of this new, unique Series is to offer readable, teachable "thinking frames" on today's social problems and social issues by leading scholars. These are available for view on http://routledge.customgateway.com/routledge-social-issues.html.

For instructors teaching a wide range of courses in the social sciences, the Routledge *Social Issues Collection* now offers the best of both worlds: originally written short texts that provide "overviews" to important social issues *as well as* teachable excerpts from larger works previously published by Routledge and other presses.

As an instructor, click to the website to view the library and decide how to build your custom anthology and which thinking frames to assign. Students can choose to receive the assigned materials in print and/or electronic formats at an affordable price.

Available

Body Problems
Running and Living Long in a Fast-Food Society
Ben Agger

Sex, Drugs, and Death
Addressing Youth Problems in American Society
Tammy Anderson

The Stupidity Epidemic
Worrying About Students, Schools, and America's Future
Joel Best

Empire Versus Democracy
The Triumph of Corporate and Military Power
Carl Boggs

Contentious Identities
Ethnic, Religious, and Nationalist Conflicts in Today's World
Daniel Chirot

The Future of Higher Education
Dan Clawson and Max Page

Waste and Consumption
Capitalism, the Environment, and the Life of Things
Simonetta Falasca-Zamponi

Rapid Climate Change
Causes, Consequences, and Solutions
Scott G. McNall

The Problem of Emotions in Societies
Jonathan H. Turner

Outsourcing the Womb
Race, Class, and Gestational Surrogacy in a Global Market
France Winddance Twine

Changing Times for Black Professionals
Adia Harvey Wingfield

Forthcoming

Due Process Denied: Detentions and Deportations in the United States

Tanya Golash-Boza

University of Kansas

Routledge
Taylor & Francis Group

NEW YORK AND LONDON

First published 2012
by Routledge
711 Third Avenue, New York, NY 10017

Simultaneously published in the UK
by Routledge
2 Park Square, Milton Park, Abingdon, Oxon OX14 4RN

Routledge is an imprint of the Taylor & Francis Group, an informa business

Library of Congress Cataloging in Publication Data
Golash-Boza, Tanya Maria.
Due process denied : detentions and deportations in the United States / Tanya
Golash-Boza.
p. cm. — (Framing 21st century social issues)
1. Illegal aliens—United States. 2. Immigration enforcement—United States.
3. Deportation—United States. I. Title.
KF4800.G65 2011
342.7308'2—dc23
2011039542

ISBN13: 978-0-415-50930-5 (pbk)
ISBN13: 978-0-203-12392-8 (ebk)

Typeset in Garamond and Gill Sans
by EvS Communication Networx, Inc.

University Readers (www.universityreaders.com): Since 1992, University
Readers has been a leading custom publishing service, providing reasonably priced,
copyright-cleared, course packs, custom textbooks, and custom publishing services
in print and digital formats to thousands of professors nationwide. The Routledge
Custom Gateway provides easy access to thousands of readings from hundreds of
books and articles via an online library. The partnership of University Readers and
Routledge brings custom publishing expertise and deep academic content together
to help professors create perfect course materials that is affordable for students.

Printed and bound in the United States of America by Publishers Graphics,
LLC on sustainably sourced paper.

Contents

Series Foreword

The world in the early 21st century is beset with problems—a troubled economy, global warming, oil spills, religious and national conflict, poverty, HIV, health problems associated with sedentary lifestyles. Virtually no nation is exempt, and everyone, even in affluent countries, feels the impact of these global issues.

Since its inception in the 19th century, sociology has been the academic discipline dedicated to analyzing social problems. It is still so today. Sociologists offer not only diagnoses; they glimpse solutions, which they then offer to policy makers and citizens who work for a better world. Sociology played a major role in the civil rights movement during the 1960s in helping us to understand racial inequalities and prejudice, and it can play a major role today as we grapple with old and new issues.

This series builds on the giants of sociology, such as Weber, Durkheim, Marx, Parsons, Mills. It uses their frames, and newer ones, to focus on particular issues of contemporary concern. These books are about the nuts and bolts of social problems, but they are equally about the frames through which we analyze these problems. It is clear by now that there is no single correct way to view the world, but only paradigms, models, which function as lenses through which we peer. For example, in analyzing oil spills and environmental pollution, we can use a frame that views such outcomes as unfortunate results of a reasonable effort to harvest fossil fuels. "Drill, baby, drill" sometimes involves certain costs as pipelines rupture and oil spews forth. Or we could analyze these environmental crises as inevitable outcomes of our effort to dominate nature in the interest of profit. The first frame would solve oil spills with better environmental protection measures and clean-ups, while the second frame would attempt to prevent them altogether, perhaps shifting away from the use of petroleum and natural gas and toward alternative energies that are "green."

These books introduce various frames such as these for viewing social problems. They also highlight debates between social scientists who frame problems differently. The books suggest solutions, both on the macro and micro levels. That is, they suggest what new policies might entail, and they also identify ways in which people, from the ground level, can work toward a better world, changing themselves and their lives and families and providing models of change for others.

Readers do not need an extensive background in academic sociology to benefit from these books. Each book is student-friendly in that we provide glossaries of terms for the uninitiated that are keyed to bolded terms in the text. Each chapter ends with questions for further thought and discussion. The level of each book is accessible to undergraduate students, even as these books offer sophisticated and innovative analyses.

Tanya Golash-Boza addresses the burning issues of detention and deportation, topics that acquire added significance in an age of globalization, when national borders become more permeable. Due process protections are among the most important constitutional protections in the United States, yet they do not apply to non-citizens facing detention and deportation. In her book, she describes the consequences of this lack of due process through the stories of deportees and detainees. People who have lived nearly all of their lives in the United States have been detained and deported for minor crimes, without regard for constitutional limits on disproportionate punishment. The court's insistence that deportation is not punishment does not align with the experiences of deportees. For many, deportation is one of the worst imaginable punishments. This is an important contribution to an emerging literature on nation, identity, and legality.

Preface

The order of deportation is not a punishment for crime.
U.S. Supreme Court in *Fong Yue Ting v. United States*, 149 U.S. 698 (1893)

Deportation is a drastic penalty equivalent to banishment or exile.
U.S. Supreme Court in *Fong Haw Tan v. Phelan*, 333 U.S. 6 (1948)

In our society, liberty is the norm, and detention prior to trial or without trial is the carefully limited exception.
U.S. Supreme Court in *United States v. Salerno*, 481 U.S. 739 (1987)

Due process protections are among the most important constitutional protections in the United States, a land of immigrants. It is thus remarkable that due process protections do not apply to immigrants facing detention and deportation, as immigration proceedings in the United States are civil, not criminal, in nature. The purpose of the due process clause is to ensure that the government does not act arbitrarily, and that any person facing a denial of life, liberty, or property is given a fair trial and the right to appeal the decision. These rights are at the core of the U.S. Constitution and of the moral fabric of the United States.

In the United States, deportation is not punishment—it is the civil penalty for violating the Immigration and Nationality Act (INA). People who have lived nearly all of their lives in the United States have been deported for possession of small amounts of marijuana and shoplifting, without regard for the constitutional limits on disproportionate punishment. People convicted of certain crimes classified as aggravated felonies face "mandatory deportation without a discretionary hearing where family and community ties can be considered." The court's insistence that deportation is not punishment does not align with the experiences of deportees. For people who have spent decades in the United States and have developed strong community and family ties to the United States, deportation is one of the worst imaginable punishments. *Due Process Denied* makes clear the consequences of this lack of due process through stories of deportees who have been banished from the United States.

In U.S. law, immigration detention is not intended to have the punitive consequences that prisons have, yet many people in detention experience being detained as a denial of life, liberty, and/or property. Legal permanent residents of the United States often spend months in immigration detention as they undergo lengthy deportation proceedings. Many are ineligible for bond, despite their strong ties to the United States and scant criminal history. In some cases, the burden of proof is on the detainee. Many times, the judge and the jailer are one and the same. In these and other ways, the detention of non-citizens violates due process protections.

Using personal narratives and case studies, *Due Process Denied* explains how people held in immigration detention and facing deportation often do not have due process protections.

1:   Introduction

~~~~~~~~

J oe Velasquez was at a party in 1980 when an undercover police officer approached him and asked where he could purchase drugs. Joe was in his early twenties at the time and knew of a person who might have some cocaine. He pointed the undercover agent to the drug dealer. This action led to Joe getting a drug conviction and five years of probation. Once that was over, Joe never got into trouble with the law again. He married a U.S. citizen, had three children, and opened up a sandwich shop in Philadelphia. He figured his past was behind him. It would have been, had Joe been a U.S. citizen.

Joe, however, was a Panamanian citizen, and **legal permanent resident** of the United States. Moreover, in 1996 the laws changed, meaning that, in 1998, at the age of 52, Joe Velasquez was arrested and taken to Hudson County Jail, where he was to be **detained** until he could be **deported** to Panama. A change in deportation laws in 1996 meant Joe faced **mandatory deportation** to Panama, a country he had not lived in since he was five years old.[1]

Joe Velasquez's case is emblematic of the lack of **due process** in **deportation** proceedings. Due process refers to the establishment of appropriate procedures prior to subjecting anyone to punishment or the deprivation of liberty, and Joe did not have the procedural protections normally accorded in criminal proceedings. This lack of procedural protections was significant in three ways:

1. As a non-citizen facing deportation, Joe did not have the right to a bond hearing to determine whether or not he should be detained.
2. His detention and deportation were mandatory. If the **immigration judge** had had the opportunity to weigh all of the equities in Joe's case through such a review, he might have found that Joe's three decades in the United States, family ties, and evidence of rehabilitation meant he did not deserve permanent exile.
3. Joe's deportation order was retroactive: although his 1980 drug conviction did not lead to deportation when he was convicted, a change in laws meant he could be ordered deported retroactively.

---

1 Joe Velasquez's case is described in the documentary film, *Abandoned: The Betrayal of America's Immigrants.*

The purpose of the due process clause is to ensure that the government does not act arbitrarily, and that any person facing a denial of life, liberty, or property is given a fair trial and the right to appeal the decision (Alderman and Kennedy 1991). Legal scholar John Vile contends that "the clause prohibiting the government from depriving anyone of 'life, liberty, or property, without due process of law' is one of the most important in the entire Constitution" (Vile 2006). This aspect of U.S. law, like many other aspects, can be traced back to the 1215 *Magna Carta*, Chapter 39 of which states: "No freeman shall be captured or imprisoned or disseised[2] or outlawed or exiled or in any way destroyed, nor will we go against him or send against him, except by the lawful judgment of his peers or by the law of the land" (*Magna Carta* online). The due process clause of the U.S. Constitution goes farther than the *Magna Carta* insofar as it places emphasis on the way the law is enforced, noting that the process through which a person could be deprived of life, liberty, or land must be fair and impartial.

The reason Joe did not have the right to due process in his deportation proceedings is that deportation proceedings in the United States are civil, not criminal, in nature. And, the due process clause is limited to criminal proceedings. Thus, although the rights to due process and a fair trial are fundamental to the democratic tradition in the United States, these procedural protections are denied to non-citizens in deportation proceedings. Non-citizens can be arrested without a warrant, detained without a bond hearing, and deported without due process.

This book explores this contradiction: deportation proceedings are technically civil in nature, and thus are not included in the due process clause, yet many people experience being detained and deported as punitive. Immigrants in **detention** are deprived of their liberty, and those that are deported often experience their detention as exile from the only country they have known. *Due Process Denied* explains how and why constitutional protections are denied to non-citizens and exposes some of the human rights violations engendered in the detention and deportation regimes of the 21st-century United States.

Who Gets Detained?

The **immigration detention** system is a complex of Department of Homeland Security (DHS) detention centers, county and city jails, and privately owned prisons used to hold people awaiting immigration trials or deportations. In 2009, DHS detained about 380,000 people at 350 different facilities, at a cost of more than $1.7 billion

---

2 Disseisin, disseizin—The act or fact of disseising; privation of seisin; usually, the wrongful dispossession (by forcible entry or otherwise) of the lands, etc. of another (retrieved April 25, 2011 from: http://www.magnacartaplus.org/magnacarta/definitions.htm#disseise).

for 2009 alone. DHS detains, on average, 32,000 people per day, at a cost of about $122 per person, per day (Detention Watch Network 2008; National Immigrant Justice Center 2010). Over the past 30 years, we have witnessed a dramatic surge in the number of detainees. The first notable increase came with the arrival of large numbers of Cuban and Haitian immigrants in the early 1980s. The second, more substantial, increase occurred after the passage of the Illegal Immigration Reform and Immigrant Responsibility Act of 1996 (IIRIRA) (Dow 2004). This law required the detention of legal permanent residents convicted of an array of crimes and expanded the grounds on which **asylum seekers** were to be detained (Fragomen 1997). The third surge came with the creation of the DHS in 2003. The infusion of funds into DHS has allowed it to enforce immigration laws more aggressively and to house more detainees. In 1973, the Immigration and Naturalization Service (INS) detained a daily average of 2,370 migrants. By 1980, this had gone up to 4,062. By 1994, the daily average was 5,532; it was about 20,000 in 2001; and, in 2008, Immigration and Customs Enforcement (ICE) detained an average of 33,400 migrants a day (Golash-Boza 2012). These detainees are not serving time for any criminal law violations. Instead, they are civil detainees awaiting trial or deportation.

As the immigration detention system is not part of the criminal justice system, the rights accorded to suspected and convicted criminals do not apply to detainees. For

---

Administrative Removal: The removal of an alien under a DHS order based on the determination that the individual has been convicted of an aggravated felony or certain other serious criminal offenses. The alien may be removed without a hearing before an immigration court.

Deportable Alien: An alien who has been admitted into the United States but who is subject to removal pursuant to provisions of the Immigration and Nationality Act (INA § 237).

Detention: The seizure and incarceration of an alien in order to hold him/her while awaiting judicial or legal proceedings or return transportation to his/her country of citizenship.

Inadmissible Alien: An alien seeking admission into the United States who is ineligible to be admitted according to the provisions of the Immigration and Nationality Act (INA § 212).

Removal: The compulsory and confirmed movement of an inadmissible or deportable alien out of the United States based on an order of removal. An alien who is removed has administrative or criminal consequences placed on subsequent reentry owing to the fact of the removal.

Expedited Removal: (INA § 235(b)) A process by which DHS may order an alien removed. This requires a finding that the alien is inadmissible pursuant to INA § 212(a)(6)(C) or (a)(7) based on having fraudulent documents or not having proper entry documents. Such aliens are generally removed without further hearing or review.

Withdrawal: An arriving alien's voluntary retraction of an application for admission to the United States in lieu of a removal.

Figure 1.1 Definitions of immigration enforcement terms.
Source: U.S. Department of Homeland Security (2009)

example, the burden of proof lies with the detainee to establish that he or she is in fact a citizen, or has other reasons which render him or her eligible to remain in the United States. Many non-citizens are detained for years before being able to prove that they are legally eligible to remain in the United States (Dow 2004).

Who Gets Deported?

Deportation is the forced **removal** of a non-citizen from the United States. People can be ordered deported for a specified period of time, or for life. A person is deported once an immigration judge determines they are ineligible to remain in the United States and orders them removed from the country. The process through which this determination is made does not include the due process protections given to people charged with criminal law violations. People facing deportation do not have the right to a jury trial, to appointed counsel, or to a fair and balanced hearing. In 2009, 393,289 people were deported from the United States—an average of over 1,000 people a day. Like detentions, deportations have soared in the aftermath of the 1996 legislation and the creation of the Department of Homeland Security (DHS) (U.S. Department of Homeland Security 2010).

Non-citizens in the United States can be deported on criminal or non-criminal grounds. In fiscal year (FY) 2009, 128,345 people were deported on criminal grounds and 264,944 on non-criminal grounds (U.S. Department of Homeland Security 2010). People deported on non-criminal grounds are non-citizens who lack the proper documentation to be in the United States, or who have violated the terms of their visas. People deported on criminal grounds are those who been convicted of a crime that renders them deportable. The former group of people is known as "**undocumented migrants**" or "**illegal aliens**." DHS refers to the second group as "**criminal aliens**." About 10 percent of the 897,099 people deported on criminal grounds between April 1, 1997, and August 1, 2007 (87,844) were legal permanent residents of the United States, and about 20 percent (179,038) were legally present in the United States as either legal permanent residents, **asylees**, **refugees**, **parolees**, or on a temporary visa (Human Rights Watch 2009). The remaining 70 percent were undocumented migrants. According to ICE reports, 30 percent of the criminal aliens deported in FY 2009 were removed for drug crimes, 16 percent for traffic offenses, and 16 percent for immigration offenses. Relatively few people were deported for violent crimes: 7 percent for assault, 2.5 percent for robbery, and 2 percent for sexual assault (U.S. Department of Homeland Security 2010). The majority of **criminal deportees** were long-term residents of the United States: half of the people deported between 1997 and 2006 on criminal grounds had spent more than 14 years in the United States (Transnational Records Access Clearinghouse 2006).

Non-citizens who are here legally and charged with a crime are afforded due process protections in the criminal justice system. However, after serving any time for the crimes they have committed, they are then handed over to the immigration law enforcement system, where they do not have the same protections. For example, a legal permanent resident convicted of a misdemeanor shoplifting offense could be sentenced to a few days in jail. After serving his time, he would be subject to mandatory detention while awaiting the outcome of his deportation trial. He could spend months or years in an immigration detention facility, much more time than for his original conviction, waiting for his removal hearing. At his removal hearing, where he would find out whether or not he would be deported from the United States, he would have no right to appointed counsel and he may not be able to present equities in his favor. If deported, he could be sent to the land of his or even his mother's birth, even if he has no ties there whatsoever (Markowitz 2008).

Natalia, who has lived in the United States since she was two days old, faces deportation to Haiti, a country in which she has never set foot. Natalia was born in the Bahamas to a Haitian mother. Haitians born in the Bahamas are considered Haitian citizens, not Bahamians. Thus, Natalia is a Haitian citizen. Shortly after the birth of her first child, Natalia was caught stealing clothes. Because of this shoplifting charge, Natalia has been ordered deported to Haiti, a country fraught with poverty and political unrest, and whose language she does not speak (Wessler 2011).

Immigration Law and Due Process

Deportation is an administrative, not a criminal, procedure. A person can be ordered deported if they have violated provisions of the **Immigration and Nationality Act (INA)** by, for example, overstaying their visa, entering the United States without inspection, or ignoring a deportation order. None of these are crimes and there is no punishment for them. Instead, if a person is found to be in violation of the INA, they face detention and then deportation (Kanstroom 2000). The United States considers neither detention nor deportation to be punishment (see, for example, *INS v. Lopez-Mendoza* 1984). As detention and deportation are not punishment, these procedures do not require the due process protections typically accorded to criminal law enforcement. Border Patrol agents have the "authority to order the removal of aliens whom they have determined to be inadmissible, without providing for further review of such a decision" (Fragomen 1997: 445). A person seeking entry to the United States who does not qualify for admission is an **inadmissible alien**. A person who is inadmissible will either be placed in **expedited removal** proceedings or will request a **withdrawal**, meaning they voluntarily retract their request to enter the United States and are not formally removed. Instead, they undergo a **voluntary departure**.

In addition, United States law considers non-citizens who crossed the border without inspection to be *seeking entry* to the United States, even if they are currently residing in the United States. Non-citizens who enter the United States without inspection are considered to have never "made a legitimate entry into the U.S." and are thus "treated extra-territorially as subjects standing at U.S. border points of entry and [are] made subject to summary exclusion by federal immigration officers without defense or relief through the courts" (Coleman 2007: 60). An undocumented migrant can be considered to be seeking entry in all immigration proceedings.

A person who is seeking entry to the United States is usually not considered a person before the law in the United States, and is thus not entitled to constitutional protections. After all, if they are seeking entry, they are not actually in the United States, and not subject to the laws of the land. For example, if a person residing in another country wishes to enter the United States, they present documentation which shows their eligibility for entry to an immigration inspector at the border. That inspector will make a decision with regard to the admissibility of the non-citizen. If the person is denied entry by the immigration inspector, he or she cannot appeal that decision, nor can he or she demand further review. The decision of the immigration inspector is final. This provision makes sense when we consider the right of the United States to determine who can and cannot enter this country, and if we presume that a person seeking entry to the United States has no stake in this nation. However, there are many cases where this determination is not as clear. Some people seeking entry actually do have a stake in this country. This is the case, for example, when returning non-citizens wish to re-enter, when asylum seekers are fleeing persecution, and when immigration inspectors interrogate people already present in the United States. In some cases, non-citizens living in the United States are technically considered to be seeking admission to the United States and are treated accordingly under the law, even if they have strong ties to this country, and even if they are already in the United States.

Immigration law distinguishes between non-citizens who are: 1) inadmissible to the United States, 2) eligible for deportation, and 3) legally eligible to be in this country. The first category—inadmissible aliens—includes non-citizens who do not reside within U.S. borders, those that hope to return to the United States, and even those who are presently living in the United States. This is where it gets complicated: if you are living in the United States you can be considered to be seeking entry and thus judged inadmissible.

Those people who are considered to be seeking entry to the United States can be subject to expedited removal, a streamlined process of deportation. Expedited removal means that an immigration officer can order a person deported without any further hearing or review. To avoid being subjected to expedited removal, a non-citizen must show that he or she has been present in the United States for at least two years, has a claim to lawful status in the United States, or fears persecution upon return to his or her home country (Grable 1997–98).[3] An expedited removal can be carried out by an immigration officer. In contrast, non-citizens who are deemed eligible for deportation, as opposed to expedited removal, have a right to a hearing before an immigration judge.

Formal removal involves more procedural protections than expedited removal, but fewer than criminal procedures. In these cases, non-citizens have the right to submit evidence of their right to remain in the United States, except when they have been convicted of an aggravated felony. Non-citizens convicted of aggravated felonies can be subject to an **administrative removal**, meaning they do not have a hearing before an immigration court. Once ordered deported, people have the right to appeal the case. They do not, however, have the right to appointed counsel or to a jury trial. Moreover, since these proceedings are civil not criminal, Congress can change the laws at any time, and even can implement retroactive clauses. Thus, a person can be convicted of an offense in 1988 that did not render him or her deportable at that time. Congress, however, can change the law such that it applies retroactively and a non-citizen can face deportation in 1998 for a 1988 conviction (Markowitz 2008).

Any non-citizen living in the United States could face deportation, as the laws governing her presence can change at any time. Thus, a person who is considered legally eligible to be in the United States today could see their status change at any moment. And, the rules governing their permission to remain in the United States are not subject to the same scrutiny as those related to the handling of people convicted of crimes.

An undocumented migrant who has lived in the United States for 30 years, and who has U.S. citizen children and grandchildren, can be ordered deported without due process. He has fewer rights at his trial than does a murder suspect. Unlike murder suspects, he can be arrested without a warrant. He may be able to appeal his case by applying for cancellation of removal, but may be detained while doing so, has no right to appointed counsel, must bear the burden of proof, and may have no right to **judicial review**. Most of the evidence he may wish to present—such as his ties to the United States and his lack of ties to his home country—will be inadmissible. As deportation is not punishment, immigration trials are not under the purview of the criminal justice system and people facing deportation have few procedural protections (Kanstroom 2000).

In this book, I outline the array of problems associated with the current lack of due process. My reasons for this are twofold: 1) To expose the contradictions associated

---

3 Also note, this provision was legislated with IIRIRA in 1996, yet has not been fully implemented. The present practice is to use expedited removal only in those cases where a person has been found within 100 miles of the border and has been in the United States for less than 14 days (Siskin and Wasem 2005) (http://trac.syr.edu/immigration/library/P13.pdf).

with an absence of due process in a country which holds constitutional protections so dearly; and 2) To discourage further rolling back these protections in any effort to enhance the effectiveness of current immigration policy enforcement efforts.

"Deport all Illegals" and Due Process Concerns

There are many reasons why a non-citizen may not have the legal documentation to be in the United States. People lack authorization to be in the United States because they entered illegally, their visa has expired, they violated the conditions of their visa, or their visa application has been denied. Their crime, then, is either "entry without inspection," "visa overstay," or ignoring a deportation order. These legal infractions are about as serious as driving without a license, jaywalking, or failure to report to jury duty, depending on the sort of comparison you wish to draw.

There are about 10 million people in the United States who lack authorization to be in this country. Some of these people are in the process of legalizing; others are waiting for a key life event that will permit them to legalize; and still others will never be able to gain legal status, because of more than one illegal entry, immigration fraud, or a host of other legal infractions. Given that "illegality" is a status one can move in and out of, it is not accurate to refer to people as "illegals." In addition, it is grammatically incorrect to use "illegal" as a noun. Instead, we can speak of a person illegally entering the United States or violating the terms of their visa. Throughout this text, I refer to people without proper documentation to be in the United States as "undocumented migrants."

One reason for the lack of due process in immigration law enforcement is that the process must be streamlined in order to process the millions of immigration cases that the Department of Homeland Security must deal with each year. A concerted effort to apprehend and process more non-citizens would put even more pressure on this over-burdened system. With ICE's current annual budget of $6 billion plus Customs and Border Patrol (CBP)'s budget of $10 billion, DHS is able to deport about 400,000 non-citizens each year. However, there are 10 million undocumented migrants currently in the country, and many legally present migrants who have been convicted of crimes that might render them deportable. Removing all of them is impossible under the current system and would require further scaling back the slim due process protections that non-citizens facing deportation currently have.

Overall, with about 10 million undocumented migrants and 11 million legal permanent residents in the United States, there are about 21 million people who live in the United States, yet do not have U.S. citizenship (Immigration Policy Institute 2009). To deny such a large swath of the U.S. population fundamental constitutional protections is a serious matter indeed. The United States is, after all, a land of immigrants.

DISCUSSION QUESTIONS

1. What is the due process clause and why is it important?
2. Why doesn't the due process clause apply in immigration proceedings?
3. What is immigration detention?
4. What is deportation?
5. Why does the author say that deportation is a civil, not a criminal, procedure?
6. What are some of the procedural protections afforded to criminal suspects that are not afforded to people facing deportation?

II: Immigration Detention
Prison by Another Name

><~~~*~~~<

Joseph Dantica thought he might have trouble after United Nations (UN) troops entered the premises of his church in Haiti in 2004. It became clear that he would have serious issues when a UN soldier shot a local gang member from his premises. He fled the church where he had preached for over three decades, and by the time the gang members came looking for Dantica, the elderly Haitian minister was gone. As soon as he was able to, Dantica boarded a plane to Miami.

When Dantica arrived at the Miami airport, instead of showing his valid tourist visa, he told the immigration inspector that he would like to apply for temporary asylum, as he feared for his life in Haiti. Dantica knew he would be staying longer than the 30 days his visa allowed, and did not want to misrepresent himself. Dantica was not aware that this request would land him behind bars. ICE routinely detains asylum seekers at the border. The immigration inspector who interviewed Dantica decided to place this elderly preacher in Miami's infamous Krome Detention Center. For Dantica, this decision was fatal.

At Krome, the staff took Dantica's medicine away from him, and gave him replacements. On his second day in immigration detention, Dantica began to experience stomach pains and complained to the officials. They initially dismissed his claims, and denied his requests to see his family in Miami. When the 91-year-old Joseph Dantica began to have a seizure and vomit shot out of his mouth and his eyes rolled back into his head, Dantica's lawyer requested a humanitarian parole so that he could be taken to a hospital and be with his family. The medic from Krome responded that he thought that Dantica was faking. He nevertheless allowed Dantica to be taken to the hospital, in shackles. Twenty-four hours after arriving in the emergency room, Joseph Dantica was seen by a physician. Later that evening, he was pronounced dead. Despite his family's pleas to see him at Krome and at the hospital, they were denied and Dantica died alone, five days after having arrived in the United States. The autopsy report showed that he "died from acute and chronic pancreatitis, … for which he was never screened, tested, diagnosed or treated while he was at Jackson Memorial Hospital" (Danticat 2007). Krome Detention Center is part of a vast complex of jails and prisons where non-citizens are held while awaiting immigration trial and deportation. Unlike prison, you cannot be sentenced to a fixed amount of time. Immigration detention is where non-citizens await immigration hearings once they have completed any prison or jail sentences. Legal scholars Patel and Jawetz explain, "[i]mmigrant detainees are not convicted prisoners. Rather they are civil detainees held pursuant to civil immigration laws" (Patel and Jawetz 2007).

The distinction between convicted prisoners and immigrant detainees is important because the United States Department of Justice (DoJ) is obliged to provide an array of protections to criminal suspects. People arrested and charged with criminal offenses in the United States have the opportunity to challenge their imprisonment before a court and the DoJ provides them with legal counsel if they cannot afford it. People held by DHS, however, do not have the same rights and safeguards as criminal suspects do in the United States. Immigrant detention is preventative, not punitive, meaning that DHS can detain people only in order to ensure that they are deported or to make sure that they are available for their removal hearing. Because immigrant detention is not punitive, the due process protections afforded to criminal suspects do not apply.

The Fifth Amendment of the United States Constitution provides for the right not to "be deprived of life, liberty or property without due process of law." In a recent Supreme Court decision, it was noted that "[f]reedom from imprisonment—from government custody, detention, or other forms of physical restraint—lies at the heart of the liberty that [the Due Process] Clause protects" (*Zadvydas v. Davis* 2001: 690). According to the U.S. Constitution, this right to liberty can only be denied through procedural and substantive due process. Moreover, preventative detention must be justified by showing that the detainee poses a flight risk or danger to society (*Zadvydas v. Davis* 2001).

The framers of the United States Constitution found the deprivation of liberty to be a very serious denial of freedom. For this reason, they included two critical protections in the Constitution: due process and habeas corpus. Together, these protections "ensure that the authority to detain must be exercised according to law, and must be subject to judicial review" (Cole 2002: 1008). In this vein, legal scholar David Cole argues "when the government takes an individual into custody, it must do so pursuant to fair procedures that afford adequate notice and a meaningful opportunity to respond, and it must have a legitimate substantive reason for the detention. The writ of habeas corpus in turn ensures that individuals will have recourse to a court that challenges the legality of their detention" (1009). The writ of habeas corpus refers to the right of a detained person to be brought before a judge.

Despite the centrality of due process and habeas corpus protections to legal frameworks in the United States, the current system of immigration detention violates these procedural protections in three critical ways: 1) The burden of proof is often on the detainee; 2) Detainees can be denied bond hearings; and 3) The judge and the jailer are sometimes the same. DHS justifies the detention of non-citizens as a measure necessary to ensure that they appear at immigration trials and leave the country when ordered to do so. However, DHS routinely detains people who do not seem to pose a flight risk. DHS detains people who are very likely to win their cases against deportation, people who have served in the U.S. armed forces, people who have lived in the United States for most of their lives, people who own homes and businesses in the United States, people, such as Joseph Dantica, who are ill and frail, and people with U.S. citizen parents, children, and siblings. DHS even detains people who are in fact U.S. citizens, yet unable to prove this.

Detention Feels like Prison

In U.S. law, immigration detention is not prison. It is not intended to have the punitive consequences that prisons have; its primary function is to hold people awaiting a deportation hearing or their actual deportation. It is important to assess whether or not detention is punitive because the DHS does not have the authority to hold anyone punitively. Instead, detention is meant to be purely preventative. In addition, DHS is bound by international standards not to punish asylum seekers, yet DHS routinely detains asylum seekers who are awaiting trial.

It turns out that many people who have been in detention experience their detention as if it were prison. I interviewed 156 people who had been deported to the Dominican Republic, Brazil, Guatemala, and Jamaica, each of whom had been in immigration detention prior to being deported.[1] I asked each deportee to describe their experiences in immigration detention. Most of my interviewees told me that they were not physically mistreated, but that they were treated like prisoners, and as if they were in prison. Most lamented the fact that they had to spend months or years in immigration detention, even though they had either finished their jail sentences or had not been convicted of any crime. Roberto, a Guatemalan deportee, described his experiences in detention to me:

> TGB: How many months were you detained?
> ROBERTO: Eleven [months] and three in Houston. They do not punish you, because they will not hit you. The thing is, they do punish you hard, though,

---

1 Between December 2008 and January 2011, I conducted 156 interviews with deportees in their countries of origin: Jamaica, Brazil, Dominican Republic, and Guatemala. I used snowball sampling and key informants to find interviewees in each country. I obtained a sample that closely resembles the overall deportee population in each country. I selected interviewees who had spent varying lengths of time in the United States, who were deported on criminal and non-criminal grounds, who had served varying prison sentences, and who had gone to the United States at various ages. The interviews ranged in length from 20 minutes to more than two hours, and were all audio-recorded, transcribed, and coded. The names of the interviewees presented herein are pseudonyms.

with words. …. The prison sentences are difficult. Who wants to be in jail so that they can just keep punishing you? If you take a little piece of food, you go to the hole. If you don't put your shirt on right, you go to the hole or they take away your telephone privileges. And, when the U.S. marshals take you, they chain you up, as if you were a criminal.

Roberto also described being taken out of detention to be put on a plane back to Guatemala. He explains what happened when he was walking toward the plane.

When I turned around, you know what one of them did to me? He went "bam" right on my head when I turned around. I told him to get a grip, because I am not a criminal. I was not doing anything [wrong]. … He told me that he was going to take me back to Louisiana or Houston, just because of that. I do not want to go through that again. I was in there for 14 months and you almost go crazy in there. I saw people who went crazy in there. I am just talking about immigration detention. We are not talking about prison.

Roberto, like many people who have been detained by immigration authorities in the United States, experienced the immigration detention center as similar to prison. The food is similar to prison food. The level of control they have over your day is similar to that of prison. And, as Roberto describes above, immigrant detainees are transported around the United States and out of the United States in chains, like prisoners.

Innocent until Proven Guilty?

Under U.S. law, the presumption of innocence is a legal right in any criminal trial. This means that the prosecution has the burden of proof and must present compelling evidence that a person is guilty. In contrast, ICE agents are authorized to detain non-citizens whom they believe to be inadmissible or deportable. The burden of proof lies with the detained person to prove they have the legal right to remain in the United States. ICE has the right to detain non-citizens to determine their eligibility to remain in the United States. It does not have the authority to detain U.S. citizens.

The question of who is a U.S. citizen, however, is not as straightforward as it may seem. You can be a U.S. citizen by *jus solis*—being born on U.S. territory, *jus sanguinis*—by being born abroad to a U.S. citizen, or **derivative citizenship**—through your parents becoming U.S. citizens before you turn 18 years old. Almost everyone born on U.S. territory is a U.S. citizen, making *jus solis* fairly straightforward. However, citizenship can be very complex when we consider derivative citizenship or even *jus sanguinis* for people born outside the United States. In those cases, the rules can be confusing and change over time. For this reason, many people are U.S. citizens and do not know they are. A Haitian friend of mine, for example, recounted to me that she applied for **naturalization** only to find out that she had automatically become a citizen when her parents became U.S. citizens when she was 15. In addition, some people think they are U.S. citizens, yet they are not. For example, Vincent, a legal permanent resident and native of Guatemala, thought he was a citizen because his mother became a citizen before he turned 18. He did not find out he was not until it was too late.

In 2007, Vincent was convicted of driving without a license, and sentenced to six weekends in jail. On his last weekend in jail, when he expected to be released, Vincent was handed over to immigration officials, and placed in immigration detention. Vincent had no idea he could be deported: he thought he was a U.S. citizen. He had lived in the United States since he was six years old, and his mother became a U.S. citizen when he was 15. She did not apply for Vincent to become a citizen, likely because she assumed that her citizenship ensured his as well. Later, they would find that it did not. As Vincent's mother was still married to his father, and his father was not a U.S. citizen, he did not automatically become a citizen with his mother's naturalization, even though his parents were no longer living together. Vincent was deported from the land he called home because he and his mother were unaware of a relatively obscure rule in naturalization law—that if parents are legally married, both have to become citizens to confer automatic citizenship on their child. Vincent thought he was a U.S. citizen until he was placed in removal proceedings and discovered he was not.

As a legal permanent resident, Vincent was subject to deportation after being convicted of a criminal offense. In 1999, Vincent was caught selling ecstasy to an undercover agent and was given a five-year suspended sentence. After his conviction, Vincent decided to straighten up and found a stable job at Whole Foods. He was doing well for himself, earning a $55,000 annual income, and continuing to move up in the company. He had his second daughter in 2004, and got custody of her when he separated from her mother. When he was deported in 2008 to Guatemala, he left his mother and two children behind.

If the Department of Homeland Security places you in removal proceedings, and you claim to be a U.S. citizen, the burden of proof is on you to prove this fact. ICE is not required to provide clear and convincing evidence that you are not a citizen. Instead, you must substantiate your claim to citizenship. This is not always easy: a 2006 survey by the Brennan Institute for Justice indicated that as many as 7 percent of U.S. citizens—13 million people—do not have ready access to proof of their citizenship, as they could not easily produce their passports, naturalization papers, or birth certificates. If ICE agents came to their doors, these people could be arrested and detained until able to provide such documentation.

Armando Vergara Ceballos finds himself in this situation. Ceballos entered the United States legally at the age of eight. He became a naturalized citizen in 1996, but subsequently misplaced his naturalization certificate. He was convicted of robbery, and placed in removal proceedings, because legal permanent residents with criminal convictions face deportation from the United States. He protested that he had become a U.S. citizen a decade earlier, and thus could not be deported. However, as he was unable to produce his naturalization certificate, and DHS did not have a record of his naturalization, he is required to remain in detention until he is able to prove his status as a U.S. citizen (*Casas-Castrillon v. Lockyer* 2007). Ceballos has already paid his debt to society for his criminal conviction. Instead of being released as a U.S. citizen should be, he is being held by DHS, as a suspected non-citizen, until he is able to prove his citizenship status, or until he is deported. The burden of proof is on Ceballos, not on the government, to prove he is a U.S. citizen.

At times, even U.S. citizens who are able to produce documentation are detained. Eduardo Caraballo, a U.S. citizen born in the United States, was detained for three days, even after showing immigration agents his valid state identification card, social security card, and birth certificate (*Huffington Post* 2010). Caraballo alleges that the immigration agents who arrested him assumed his papers were false because he looks Mexican. He was released only after his mother contacted Congressman Luis Gutierrez, who spoke out on his behalf. Again, the burden of proof was on Caraballo to prove that he was in fact a U.S. citizen. The agents who held him had no clear evidence that he was not a citizen. Nevertheless, they held him in detention until he could prove otherwise.

Jailed without Bond

In the criminal justice system, a police officer can arrest a person if they have reasonable suspicion that they have committed a crime. The suspect must be charged with a crime and have a bond hearing within 72 hours. These same protections do not apply to people in immigration proceedings. Once an immigration agent arrests a person, ICE will make an initial custody determination. If the person has just arrived in the United States, they may be subject to mandatory detention, and may not have access to a bond hearing. If the person is living in the United States and has a criminal conviction, they also may be subject to mandatory detention and have no option to be released before their trial. Mandatory detention eliminates the possibility of a bond hearing.

The question of whether or not ICE detainees merit bond hearings was recently heard in Supreme Court in the case of *Demore v. Kim* (2007). This 2003 case revolved around the question of whether non-citizens convicted of crimes should be held in detention while awaiting their deportation proceedings on a mandatory basis or if these non-citizens should be given individualized bond hearings to determine whether or not they pose a flight risk. Kim, who had been a legal permanent resident of the United States since he was a small child, argued that he should have had the right to a hearing before an impartial official. Chief Justice Rehnquist responded that "the Government may constitutionally detain **deportable aliens** during the limited period necessary for their removal proceedings" and concluded that he did not require a hearing. Rehnquist further argued that detention during removal proceedings is acceptable, in part because these proceedings are typically not lengthy (*Demore v. Kim* 2007). Justice Souter, however, dissented, arguing that non-citizens are persons before the law, and should be accorded due process. Souter cites a 1987 Supreme Court decision, in which the Chief Justice wrote: "[i]n our society liberty is the norm, and detention prior to trial or without trial is the carefully limited exception" (Souter 2003). For non-citizens subject to removal from the United States, however, detention has become the norm, and bond hearings are the exception. In this section, we will see how asylum seekers and legal permanent residents can be detained without bond hearings.

Long-Term Residents of the United States

Legal permanent residents of the United States often spend months in immigration detention as they undergo lengthy deportation proceedings. Legal permanent residents who have been ordered deported often appeal their deportation orders and use a variety of legal mechanisms to try to remain in the United States. If an immigration judge orders a legal permanent resident to be deported, he or she can appeal the decision to the Bureau of Immigration Appeals (BIA). If the BIA affirms the deportation order, he or she can appeal to the Federal Court of Appeals. The case can even go up to the Supreme Court. This appeal process can take years, and DHS can respond with their own appeals of each decision. Many legal permanent residents remain in detention throughout this lengthy litigation process. While detained, they are unable to continue working, and thus often have great difficulty paying legal fees to retain a lawyer. In addition, their detention puts tremendous stress on their families. Detention also makes it more difficult for such people to get together the documentation they need to overturn their deportation order.

Diallo, a Guatemalan citizen, spent over two years in detention fighting his case. I met Diallo, who speaks with a strong Boston accent, in the cafeteria of the Call Center where he works in Guatemala City. His voice broke and his eyes filled with tears as he explained to me that he spent more time behind bars fighting his immigration case than his original sentence. Two and a half years in the prime of his life. Diallo, who had lived in the United States for nearly 30 years, was deported for being caught with marijuana seeds on one occasion and a marijuana cigarette on another occasion, a decade later.

Diallo moved to the United States when he was eight years old, in 1980. He and his mother sought asylum in the United States because of death threats they received in Guatemala during the civil war. They were granted asylum, and Diallo and his mother became legal permanent residents of the United States. Diallo and his mother lived in a primarily white suburb of Boston, where Diallo attended Walton

Vocational High School. Upon graduation, Diallo went to work with his uncle in shipping and construction. Shortly after graduating from high school, Diallo was arrested for driving under the influence (DUI). He was given one-year probation. In addition, the police found a few seeds of marijuana in his car, and he had to pay a $50 fine for marijuana possession. After that, Diallo stayed out of trouble for nearly a decade. But, he developed a drinking problem, and in 2000 was arrested again for driving under the influence. This time, the police found a marijuana cigarette in the car, and he had to pay a $50 fine for that. For the DUI charge, Diallo had to serve six months in prison. When he was released, he was still dealing with alcoholism, and, in 2004, was arrested again for driving while intoxicated. This time, he was given a 300-day sentence. This last time, Diallo was not actually found driving while intoxicated. He had parked his car on the side of the road and had gone go to get gas for the car when he was arrested. Although he was not driving, he was not willing to take the risk of going to trial, as he thought any sentence over one year would result in him being deported. With no family ties in Guatemala, Diallo did not want to take that risk.

When Diallo finished his sentence, instead of being released, he was sent on a plane to Louisiana, to an immigration detention facility. He was not detained on the basis of his DUI and driving while intoxicated (DWI) charges, but based on the fact that he had two prior convictions of marijuana possession. Diallo fought his deportation order, but was forced to do so from behind bars. After two and a half years in detention and over $15,000 in legal fees, Diallo discontinued the appeals process. He and his mother had exhausted their resources. In addition, his diabetic mother had to find a way to pay her own medical bills and to care for Diallo's daughter, over whom he had had custody since she was an infant. In 2008, Diallo was deported to Guatemala, a land he barely remembered, leaving his mother and daughter behind.

Elias, a Jamaican national, also told me that he decided not to continue with the appeal process because of his lengthy detention, and thus decided to leave his 11 U.S. citizen children behind and agreed to be deported to Jamaica. Elias moved to the United States when he was 13 years old, to join his mother, who had lived in the United States as a legal permanent resident for eight years. Elias arrived in Brooklyn, New York in the early 1980s. He enrolled in the eighth grade, and continued to go to school until he finished high school in 1985.

In 1986, Elias was arrested and charged with selling marijuana. He did not have to go to jail, but was ordered to pay a $50 fine. Elias avoided getting into trouble with the law after that incident. Twenty years later, in 2006, Elias agreed to take a bag across town for a friend. Elias got into the cab with the bag, and within moments, a police officer pulled the cab over and asked to see the bag. The bag turned out to have 14 rocks of crack cocaine in it. Elias was arrested, convicted, and sentenced to 18 months in prison. Elias appealed the charge, claiming the bag was not his and that he did not know that there was cocaine in the bag.

Elias was released from prison while his case was still under appeal, yet did not go home, as he was immediately transported to immigration detention. His criminal charges meant he was subject to mandatory detention. Elias spent 11 months in detention trying to get his charge overturned, as that was the only way he could avoid deportation. After 11 months in detention, however, Elias gave up the appeals process. He had lived in the United States for over 20 years. He had 11 children in the United States. He had no ties to Jamaica. However, he was tired of being incarcerated, and did not have the money to continue his appeals. Thus, he agreed to be deported.

Elias and Diallo did not exhaust their appeal options. Instead, they ran out of money to pay lawyers to help them pursue their claims and grew tired of their lengthy detention. Thus, they decided to give up the appeals process and agreed to be deported. There are many non-citizens currently in detention who have meritorious claims and may be able to overturn their deportation orders. However, the fact that the appeals process is very lengthy and costly and ICE often requires non-citizens to remain in detention while they appeal means that many non-citizens who could get their deportation orders rescinded are unwilling or unable to go through the appeals process. ICE requires many non-citizens to remain in detention while their case is being litigated, and there is no system of custody hearings in place to determine if their prolonged detention is necessary.

Many non-citizens facing deportation would have much better chances at winning their cases were they to be released from detention while appealing their cases. In fact, some people are able to withstand the prolonged detention and win their cases. Diego Miguel-Miguel is a Kakchiquel Guatemalan who fled his native country after being forced to join the guerilla movement during the bloody civil war. He managed to escape after being held captive by the guerilla movement. He made it through Mexico and to the United States, where he was able to apply for and was granted asylum in 1988. Over 10 years later, in 1999, Diego was found guilty of selling a quarter of a gram of cocaine to an undercover agent for $20. He pled guilty to the charges, spent 36 days in jail, paid $200 in fines, and was sentenced to five years of probation. Instead of being released, however, the INS placed Diego in detention and in deportation proceedings. Diego appealed his deportation order on the basis that his crime was not very serious, and his claim that he would face persecution in Guatemala (*Miguel-Miguel v. Gonzales* 2007). Diego then went through a number of back-and-forth appeals with regard to whether or not he would be deported. In 2007, his case finally reached the U.S. Court of Appeals for the Ninth Circuit in Arizona, and Diego was granted a petition for review. His case was remanded to the BIA. Diego was detained for this entire time. He spent over eight years in immigration detention while his case went through a series of very lengthy appeals. During this time, he was administratively denied release twice, and was never given a custody hearing during which he could challenge his lengthy detention.

Long-term legal permanent residents who have never been imprisoned also can be detained while awaiting their immigration trials. Amnesty International reports on the case of Mr. B., a 57-year-old lawful permanent resident who had lived in the United States since he was a teenager. In August 2003, Mr. B. pled guilty to two misdemeanors and was given probation. ICE agents arrested him at one of his visits to his probation officer in November 2003. After arresting him, ICE placed Mr. B. in detention where he was to await his removal proceedings on the basis of his criminal convictions. When Mr. B. had his trial, the immigration judge determined that his two convictions did not render him deportable, as they could not be classified as aggravated felonies. Subsequently, DHS appealed this decision. Mr. B. remained in detention throughout the lengthy appeal process. Although Mr. B. has U.S. citizen children and grandchildren and had lived in the United States for four decades, he remained in immigration detention for four years, waiting for his appeals to be processed. His two misdemeanor convictions did not lead to a prison sentence. Nevertheless, he spent four years behind bars, to ensure that he would appear at his immigration hearings and appeals (Amnesty International 2008). Mr. B. had been a legal permanent resident of the United States for nearly all of his life, and found himself caught up in the detention system after two minor infractions of the law that did not merit any jail time. Eventually, he was allowed to stay in the United States and figure out how to piece his life together after four years behind bars.

Asylum Seekers

Asylum seekers are people fleeing persecution in their home country and seeking protection in other countries. In the United States, asylum seekers must prove they have a well-founded fear that, if returned to their home country, they will be persecuted on the basis of their race, religion, nationality, membership in a particular social group, or political opinion. Non-citizens may apply for asylum at the border, after arriving in the United States, or when they are facing deportation. Under current laws, applicants for asylum must convince the receiving border inspector that they have a credible fear of persecution. Otherwise, they face expedited deportation. This process has been criticized by **refugee** advocates, since border inspectors are not fully trained for the interview process. When an asylum seeker passes the credible fear of persecution test conducted by the border inspector, their next stop is usually detention, where they must wait for their application to be processed. Some are detained for a few days, yet others are detained for years while awaiting trial.

The detention of people fleeing persecution is one of the most egregious examples of human and civil rights violations related to immigration detention. This is particularly the case because asylum seekers detained are those who have already been found to have a credible fear of persecution and must wait behind bars for a final decision. A recent study found that the average stay in detention for non-criminals was 65 days, and 121 days for people with criminal convictions (Kerwin and Yi-Ying Lin 2009). The Universal Declaration of Human Rights states that "the right to seek and enjoy asylum is a basic human right," and Human Rights Watch argues that individuals should not be punished for seeking asylum in the United States. The DHS, however, maintains that detention is not punishment; it merely ensures that asylum seekers show up for their hearings. In contrast, human rights advocates contend that the detention of asylum seekers is excessive.

Saluja Thangaraja is a Tamil native and a citizen of Sri Lanka. She was forced to flee her home in Sri Lanka and was subsequently placed in a police camp because of allegations that she was a member of the Liberation Tigers of Tamil Eelam. She was tortured and brutally beaten in this camp, and fled the country to escape persecution. She took a boat from Colombo, Sri Lanka to Mexico, and made her way to the U.S./Mexico border in 2001. She attempted to enter the United States at the San Ysidro border crossing, where she explained to an asylum officer that she was fleeing political persecution in Sri Lanka. The officer found her to have a credible fear of persecution, and she was placed in immigration detention. Saluja remained in detention while she waited for her case for asylum to be heard in immigration court, the Board of Immigration Appeals, and, finally, the U.S. Court of Appeals for the Ninth Circuit. In August 2004, after Saluja had been in immigration detention for three years appealing her case, the Ninth Circuit found that she faced a well-founded fear of persecution, and that she should not be deported to Sri Lanka, where she likely would be tortured. However, the government appealed that decision, and she had to remain in immigration detention while the appeal process took place. Saluja remained in immigration detention until March of 2006—over a year after she was granted asylum—and only after the American Civil Liberties Union (ACLU) filed a habeas petition on her behalf. Saluja was 26 years old when she was finally released after four years in detention (*Thangaraja v. Ashcroft* 2004). Notably, Saluja was eventually found to have a well-founded fear of persecution and was granted asylum. Keeping her in detention for four years until this determination could be made was excessive.

Asylum seekers who pass the initial credible fear interview are sometimes released on parole. However, the rate at which they were released declined from 66.6 percent in 2004 to 4.5 percent in 2007. In 2007, over 95 percent of asylum seekers who passed the credible fear interview were placed in detention to await their immigration hearing (Human Rights First 2009). Raymond Soeoth is an asylum seeker who was released on parole in 1999. When he and his wife arrived from Indonesia in 1999 they applied for asylum in the United States based on their fear of persecution in Indonesia due to their perceived Chinese ethnicity and Christian religion. The INS granted Soeoth and his wife employment authorization and the right to remain in the country while their case was being processed. Raymond Soeoth found work, and also trained to become a Christian pastor. He was ordained as a minister in June 2004.

Three months later, Soeoth learned that his application for asylum had been denied. He was arrested in his home and placed in immigration detention. Inside immigration detention, Raymond requested that his application be reopened and reconsidered in light of the fact that he was now a Christian minister and felt he surely would be persecuted in Indonesia for his religious faith. In March 2005, his motion was denied. He then filed a petition for review. During the time the court was deciding whether or not to hear his case, he never received a hearing to determine whether or not his detention was justified. Raymond was finally released from detention on February 12, 2007, after the ACLU helped him to file a habeas petition. At that point, he had spent over two and a half years behind bars waiting for his case to be processed (*Soeoth v. Keisler* 2007). Raymond's strong ties to his community and his role as a Christian minister could have been considered convincing evidence that he did not pose a flight risk and should not be detained. However, he was never given a bond hearing during which he could present that evidence and thereby contest his detention.

Judge and Jailer are the Same

The U.S. Constitution divides the government into three branches: Legislative, Executive, and Judicial. The Legislative Branch makes the laws. The Executive Branch enforces the laws. The Judicial Branch interprets the laws. In the case of asylum seekers, to keep with this separation of powers, we would expect that Congress would make laws governing the rights of asylum seekers, ICE would enforce the laws, and asylum seekers would be permitted to use the Judicial Branch to ensure that ICE was in keeping with the laws. However, asylum seekers must arbitrate their claims to the same body that detains them: ICE. This lack of access to the Judicial Branch represents a fundamental violation of the separation of powers.

When asylum seekers arrive in the United States, their detention is often mandatory. An asylum seeker can subsequently be released on parole. However, this decision is not made by an independent judge, but by local ICE officials. The decision as to whether or not an asylum seeker will be granted parole is made by the same body that detains them. ICE plays the role of both judge and jailer. In 2007, only 4.5 percent of parole requests were granted (Human Rights First 2009). Most asylum seekers are detained and they have no avenue to contest or appeal their detention before a judge (Inter-American Commission on Human Rights 2010). The mandatory detention of asylum seekers and the lack of an independent parole review of their detention violate this fundamental principle of U.S. democracy.

The problem of the separation of powers is not limited to asylum seekers: most non-citizens who wish to adjudicate their claims to remain in the United States never have access to the Judicial Branch. Instead, the immigration courts are housed in the Executive Branch. The **Executive Office for Immigration Review (EOIR)**, which is where immigration courts are housed, is a division of the Department of Justice (DoJ), and thus part of the Executive Branch. When an immigration judge hears an immigration case, these proceedings are part of the Executive Branch, not the Judicial Branch. It is only when an immigration case reaches the Circuit Court of Appeals that the case comes under the jurisdiction of the Judicial Branch. And, those cases are quite rare.

Alternatives to Detention

The era of mass detention will have to end if we hope to restore due process to our immigration law enforcement system. The sole justification for the detention of nearly 400,000 non-citizens every year is to ensure they show up for their trials and subsequent deportation. There are many better, less expensive, and more just ways to ensure that people show up for trials. In a recent report, Amnesty International issued a series of recommendations directed at DHS detention of immigrants and asylum seekers. They recommended that:

1. Detention should not be mandatory or the default practice.
2. Decisions to detain should be subject to judicial review.
3. DHS should ensure alternatives to detention are available, including setting affordable bond and setting up community supervision programs.
4. DHS should ensure that there are safeguards against arbitrary detention and that detainees have access to competent legal representation.

DISCUSSION QUESTIONS

1. How is immigration detention similar to prison? How is it different?
2. What does it mean when the author says "immigration detention is preventative not punitive"?
3. Why does the author contend that mandatory detention is problematic?
4. How does the separation of powers operate within immigration proceedings?
5. What is an asylum seeker?
6. What is a legal permanent resident?

III: Deportation

Banishment in the 21st Century

⮞⮞✕⮜⮜

Between 1998 and 2007, over two million people were deported from the United States. Over 100,000 of these deportees had U.S. citizen children (Office of Inspector General of the Department of Homeland Security 2009). In the year 2010 alone, nearly 400,000 people were deported—more than 50 percent more than were deported in the entire decade between 1981 and 1990. Many of the people who have been deported have been legal permanent residents. Among deportees are people who have spent nearly their whole lives in the United States, and who face deportation for relatively minor offenses.

People who migrated to the United States as children have been deported for possession of small amounts of marijuana and shoplifting, without any regard for the constitutional limits on disproportionate punishment, because deportation is not punishment—it is the civil penalty for violating the Immigration and Nationality Act (INA). Deportation is an administrative procedure applied to people who do not have the legal right to remain in the United States (Kanstroom 2000). For example, a non-citizen who commits a crime in the United States first completes any jail or prison time mandated as punishment for their crime. If that criminal conviction renders them deportable, they are detained by the DHS, and then deported upon completing their sentence.

People convicted of certain crimes classified as **aggravated felonies** face "mandatory deportation without a discretionary hearing where family and community ties can be considered" (United Nations Human Rights Council 2008: 8). Congress created the idea of an aggravated felony as part of the Anti-Drug Abuse Act of 1988 to provide harsh provisions for non-citizens convicted of murder and drugs and arms trafficking. Subsequent legislation has expanded the definition of aggravated felonies and this category now includes any crime of violence or theft offense for which the term of imprisonment is at least one year, illicit drug offenses, as well as other violations. Although the definition of an aggravated felony sounds as if it is referring to severe crimes, crimes such as illegal possession of Xanax and shoplifting baby clothes have been classified as aggravated felonies and people have faced mandatory detention and deportation as a result (Golash-Boza 2012).

The constitutional safeguards that prevail in criminal proceedings do not apply in deportation proceedings. This has severe implications in five ways.

1. People facing deportation do not have the right to a trial by jury; instead they are tried by an immigration judge. This immigration judge works for the Executive Office for Immigration Review (EOIR)—part of the Executive Branch, not the Judicial Branch. Moreover, in aggravated felony cases, deportation is mandatory and there is no judicial review.

2. The Ex Post Facto Clause does not apply; this means that a person can be deported for an offense that was not a deportable offense when it was committed, and a person can be first punished under criminal law for an offense, and then deported without being able to claim double jeopardy.

3. People facing deportation do not have the right to appointed counsel; they may pay the several thousand dollars required to obtain a lawyer, but the government does not provide a public defender to people in immigration proceedings.

4. The exclusionary rule under the Fourth Amendment does not apply; this means that any evidence can be presented against the non-citizen, no matter how it was obtained. In criminal proceedings, if evidence against a suspect was obtained in an illegal search, it is inadmissible. In deportation proceedings, the government can present any evidence it chooses.

5. The Eighth Amendment prohibition against cruel and unusual punishment does not apply. A person facing deportation cannot claim that deportation would amount to cruel and unusual punishment, or that the punishment does not fit the crime, as deportation is not punishment (Pauw 2000).

Deportation Feels like Punishment

Under current U.S. laws, deportation is not punishment. When the U.S. Constitution was written, deportation laws were not included, as there was no such thing as deportation. The precursor to deportation was banishment, which was widely used as a criminal punishment in England at the time. In fact, between 1718 and 1775, 50,000 people were expelled from Britain to the Americas as punishment. Throughout the 19th century in the United States, immigration law was left to individual states. It was not until the end of the 19th century that U.S. courts began to take the matter seriously. In 1893, there was a landmark case in the Supreme Court—*Fong Yue Ting v. United States*—which involved three Chinese nationals who claimed they deserved constitutional protections in their deportation cases. The Court held that the power to deport non-citizens was inherent in the nature of sovereignty and that constitutional protections including the right to a trial by jury did not apply (Markowitz 2010).

In the case of *Fong Yue Ting v. United States,* Justice Brewer contested this idea that the United States could deport people without a trial. Brewer stated: "Deportation is punishment. It involves first an arrest, a deprival of liberty, and second, a removal from home, from family, from business, from properties ... But punishment implies a trial: 'No person shall be deprived of life, liberty, or property without due process of law'" (Salinas 2004: 261). In a subsequent case—*Ng Fung Ho v. White*—in 1919, Justice Brandeis stated:

> To deport one who so claims to be a citizen obviously deprives him of liberty. ... It may result also in loss of both property and life; or of all that makes life worth living. Against the danger of such deprivation, without the sanction afforded by judicial proceedings, the Fifth Amendment affords protection in its guarantee of due process of law.
>
> (Salinas 2004: 247)

Despite these dissenting opinions, deportation, even of legal permanent residents, continues to be a civil matter in the United States, and continues to be exempt from constitutional protections.

As Justices Brewer and Brandeis explained, deportees often experience their deportation as punishment. The more time they live in the United States, the more it feels like a punishment and a deprivation of life and liberty. The court's insistence that deportation is not punishment does not align with the experiences of deportees. Each of the 156 deportees I interviewed felt as though their deportation was punishment, either for being in the United States illegally or for committing a crime.

O'Ryan, a Jamaican citizen, moved to the United States as a legal permanent resident when he was six years old. When he was 25 years old, O'Ryan was deported to Jamaica because of a drug conviction. When I spoke to O'Ryan, he had been in Jamaica for seven years and continued to have trouble getting adjusted to life in his birth country. He told me he understands he made mistakes, but did not see it as fair that he should pay the rest of his life for those mistakes. He doesn't see a future for himself in Jamaica, where he feels like a foreigner. He told me "I shouldn't be deported because I'm really not a bad person." For O'Ryan, deportation feels like a cruel punishment that he never had the chance to contest. His deportation was an automatic consequence of his drug conviction. He had no opportunity to explain to a judge that he grew up in the United States, that he was a college student, and that he had no ties to Jamaica.

Hazel is another Jamaican who was deported after living most of her life abroad. She told me that her life in Jamaica is hard, but that she understands that it is her punishment.

> [It's] so rough to come here and no family, nobody, I didn't know nobody. I got a little sleep-in job, they throw me out, they don't pay me. I had nothing. I suffer but

thanks be to my God, because he is a good God. He kept me. I could have been like one of the other deportees that come here and lay in the street, but I didn't. Because I know that *this was my punishment,* I come here and work, I go to school, you know? I try to live right. [emphasis added]

The deportees with whom I spoke told me that they experience their deportation as punishment. However, since deportation is technically a regulatory procedure and not a punitive procedure, non-citizens do not have the right to contest their deportation in the same way they would in their criminal trials.

1996 Laws: Due Process Denied

In 1996, Congress passed two laws that fundamentally changed the rights of all foreign-born people in the United States: the Anti-Terrorism and Effective Death Penalty Act (AEDPA) and the Illegal Immigration Reform and Immigrant Responsibility Act (IIRIRA). These laws were striking in that they eliminated judicial review of some deportation orders, required mandatory detention for many non-citizens, and introduced the potential for the use of secret evidence in certain cases. One of the most pernicious consequences of these is related to the deportation of legal permanent residents—non-citizens who have been granted legalization and have the right to remain in the United States on a permanent basis, so long as they do not violate provisions of the INA. Prior to 1996, judges were permitted to exercise discretion in deportation cases. When deciding whether or not to deport a person who had been convicted of a crime, judges could consider the immigrant's rehabilitation, remorse, family support, and ties (or lack thereof) to their country of origin. The 1996 laws took away the judge's discretionary power in aggravated felony cases.

The 1996 laws—IIRIRA and AEDPA—seem to be in conflict with an array of constitutional rights, including the Fifth and Sixth Amendments and the right to procedural due process. The Fifth Amendment to the Constitution sets out that a person shall not "be subject for the same offence to be twice put in jeopardy of life or limb." It is only by claiming that deportation is not punishment that one could argue that the U.S. government is not violating the U.S. Constitution, which indicates that a person should not be punished twice for the same crime. Legal permanent residents who are convicted of certain crimes in the United States face deportation after serving their sentences. The decision as to whether or not they are to be deported is made by an immigration judge. However, it is not technically correct to say that they are punished twice for a crime—as deportation is not punishment. The Sixth Amendment provides for the right to counsel in criminal trials, which non-citizens are denied in immigration proceedings. The retroactive nature of these laws also violates due process insofar as there is no way that a person who pled guilty to a crime in 1995 or earlier could have known that crime could be reclassified as an aggravated felony in 1996, and that he or she would face deportation as a result. Procedural due process implies that all people should know the full range of consequences of a guilty plea before entering one (Salinas 2004).

One could also argue that deportation laws discriminate on the basis of national origin. The Civil Rights Act of 1964 made it illegal to discriminate against someone on the basis of race, color, religion, national origin, or sex. Nevertheless, deportation law is discriminatory toward non-citizens. For example, if a citizen and a non-citizen both shoplift $900 worth of clothes and both are sentenced to 18 months in prison, the citizen goes free after serving his or her time, yet the non-citizen is detained and faces deportation after serving his or her time. Although the non-citizen is treated differently for the same crime, the U.S. government holds that this is not in violation of the Civil Rights Act because detention and deportation are not punishment.

The 1996 laws were particularly damaging to immigrants in three ways:

1. Deportation became mandatory in aggravated felony cases, removing the possibility for judicial review.
2. The laws were retroactive.
3. The 1996 laws criminalized illegal re-entry and made it such that a person who enters the United States illegally twice is permanently barred from re-entry and faces the possibility of doing time in federal prison.

Removing Discretion

As described above, IIRIRA and AEDPA eliminated the ability of immigration judges to exercise discretion in aggravated felony cases. In immigration proceedings, once an immigration judge determines that a person has indeed been convicted of a crime that can be classified as an aggravated felony, he or she faces mandatory and automatic deportation, no matter what the extenuating circumstances might be. The absence of discretion in aggravated felony cases means that legal permanent residents who have lived in the United States for decades, have contributed greatly to society, and have extensive family ties in the country, are subject to deportation for relatively minor crimes they may have committed years ago.

Immigration judges do not have the opportunity to take people's family and community ties into account in aggravated felony cases. Nor can judges take into account weak or non-existent linkages to their countries of birth. The only recourse that people facing deportation on aggravated felony charges have is to hire their own lawyer (often paying thousands of dollars) to argue that the charge they face is not in fact an aggravated felony. If the judge determines that the crime is indeed an aggravated felony, the defendant cannot present evidence that, for example, he or she is the sole caregiver of a disabled U.S. citizen child. Judges cannot take family ties, the needs of

U.S. citizen children, or the likelihood of rehabilitation into account in aggravated felony cases.

The U.S. Constitution does not directly address deportation. However, the U.S. government is party to two international treaties that specify how governments should handle deportations. For example, Article 13 of the International Covenant of Civil and Political Rights (ICCPR), which the United States has ratified, states,

> An alien lawfully in the territory of a State party to the present covenant may be expelled therefrom only in pursuance of a decision reached in accordance with law and shall, except when compelling reasons of national security otherwise require, be allowed to submit the reasons against his expulsion and to have his case reviewed by, and be represented for the purpose before, the competent authority or a person or persons especially designated by the competent authority.

In addition, the American Convention on Human Rights (ACHR), to which the United States is party, states, "Every person has the right to a hearing, with due guarantees and within a reasonable time, by a competent, independent and impartial tribunal, previously established by law." The absence of discretion in deportation hearings of legal permanent residents accused of aggravated felonies violates these treaties, both of which have been signed by the U.S. government.

In a groundbreaking case, the Inter-American Commission on Human Rights (IACHR) concluded in July 2010 that the United States stands in violation of Articles V, VI, VII, XVIII, and XXVI of the American Declaration. This decision was made on the basis of the deportation of two legal permanent residents: Hugo Armendariz and Wayne Smith. Hugo Armendariz was born in Mexico, yet came to the United States when he was two years old in 1972. He became a legal permanent resident in 1978, when he was eight years old. Armendariz's mother is a U.S. citizen, and he has two U.S. citizen children. Having lived nearly all of his life in the United States, he has no ties to Mexico. Nevertheless, when he was in his late twenties, Armendariz was convicted on drug charges and deported to Mexico. Wayne Smith is a citizen of Trinidad and Tobago and lived in the United States for 25 years before being ordered deported to his country of birth. The IACHR found that Smith and Armendariz deserved judicial review of their cases, and that automatic deportation was in violation of the American Declaration. The decision specified that:

> it is well-recognized under international law that a Member State must provide non-citizen residents an opportunity to present a defense against deportation based on humanitarian and other considerations … Each Member State's administrative or judicial bodies, charged with reviewing deportation orders, must be permitted to give meaningful consideration to a non-citizen resident's defense, balance it against the State's sovereign right to enforce reasonable, objective immigration

policy, and provide effective relief from deportation if merited. The United States did not follow these international norms in the present case.

(Inter-American Commission on Human Rights 2010)

The IACHR found that the United States' decision to deport Hugo Armendariz and Wayne Smith, both long-term legal permanent residents of the United States, was in violation of international standards insofar as Armendariz and Smith did not have the opportunity to present evidence of their rehabilitation, their family ties, or other equities in their favor. As legal permanent residents convicted of aggravated felonies, Armendariz and Smith were not granted judicial review of their deportation orders. In addition to violating their right to establish a family, their deportation violated the rights of their children to special protections. The best interests of their U.S. citizen children were not taken into account. The IACHR recommended that the United States "implement laws to ensure that non-citizen residents' right to family life, as protected under Articles V, VI, and VII of the American Declaration, are duly protected and given due process on a case-by-case basis in U.S. immigration removal proceedings." The United States asserted its right to sovereignty and has not resolved to change immigration laws on the basis of this decision (Inter-American Commission on Human Rights 2010).

The aggravated felony provisions create a situation where long-term legal permanent residents are unable to contest their deportation orders. This happens even when legal permanent residents have strong ties to the United States and very few ties to their country of origin. Victor is one example of such a person: he was deported to Jamaica when he was 27 years old even though he had been in the United States since he was four years old and had no family members in Jamaica. Back in Jamaica, Victor has not been able to find a job. He doesn't have any skills or connections. He survives by selling whatever he can find. He burns CDs and sells them; he sells used clothes. His mother in New York barely earns enough to get by herself, and can't afford to support him.

Victor was deported after serving time for a drug charge. Victor's mother had separated from her husband because of domestic abuse, and barely was able to make ends meet with housekeeping and babysitting jobs. Victor saw his friends making money selling marijuana, and decided to try his hand at selling marijuana as well so that he could help his mother with the bills. As a street-level seller, he was quickly caught. His first charge was possession of marijuana, and he was given three years of probation. Victor managed to stay out of trouble for a while. However, in 1996, he was caught with 50 pounds of marijuana, and was sentenced to four years in prison. He served two and a half years, and, in 1999, was deported to Jamaica.

Victor broke the law. As a legal permanent resident, he was a guest of the United States. But, does it really make sense to deport him to Jamaica? As the 1953 Presidential Commission charged with reviewing deportation orders pointed out,

> Each of the aliens is a product of our society. Their formative years were spent in the United States, which is the only home they have ever known. The countries of origin which they left ... certainly are not responsible for their criminal ways.
>
> (Morawetz 2000: 1961)

The fact that Victor's formative years were spent in the United States was not considered in his immigration hearing.

Had Victor been a citizen of the United States, he would have served his time, been released, and been able to make his choices about how to better his life in America. Instead, he was deported to a land he barely knows. Victor was eligible for citizenship. At age nine, his mother could have taken him to the INS and naturalized him. Had she become a citizen, he may have become a citizen automatically. Victor's mother probably didn't have the extra time and money to process a citizenship application. Victor could have become a citizen himself at age 18, but he did not. Like many American teenagers, he had other things on his mind. Now, he is paying dearly for his (and his mother's) failure to apply for citizenship.

O'Ryan is another legal permanent resident who was deported after being convicted of an aggravated felony. O'Ryan moved to the United States when he was six years old to join his mother and grandmother who had gone a few years before. O'Ryan graduated with honors from his junior high school, and made it into John Dewey, a competitive high school in Brooklyn. However, most of his friends were not attending school, and he slowly stopped going to classes. Instead, O'Ryan earned his General Equivalency Diploma (GED), and enrolled in Mercy College, where he was studying computer programming.

While studying at Mercy College, O'Ryan worked part-time at a series of jobs. He tried to stay out of trouble, though, because he hated the look on his mother's face whenever she heard he was getting into trouble. One evening, O'Ryan was hanging out, after spending the whole day inside with his girlfriend. A friend called to ask him to pick him up, as his car had broken down. O'Ryan agreed. On the highway, they came upon a road block. At that point, his friend told him, "Yo, I'm dirty," meaning that he had drugs with him and had not told O'Ryan. The police found the drugs, and O'Ryan was sentenced to three to nine years for drug trafficking. He chose to do boot camp, so he only spent 18 months in jail.

On the day of O'Ryan's graduation from boot camp, his mother, his girlfriend, and his newly born daughter came to the graduation. O'Ryan saw his daughter for the first time. He was expecting to go home with them and begin his life anew. But, immigration agents were waiting for him, and told him he was going to be deported.

O'Ryan had been in the country for nearly 20 years, and had no family he knew in Jamaica. O'Ryan qualified for citizenship, and, in fact, had applied when his green card expired in 1996. His mother and cousin applied at the same time. His mother's citizenship went through, and then his cousin's. So, he went to check on his citizenship. The citizenship office told him he needed to redo his fingerprints. He finally received the letter saying he should go to the swearing-in ceremony in 2001, five years later.

Unfortunately, O'Ryan had been arrested a few weeks earlier, and was in jail when his letter arrived. So, at the age of 25, O'Ryan was deported to a country he barely knew. His grandmother's sister agreed to take him in, so he is not homeless. Back in Jamaica, it has been very hard to find work, especially a permanent position. O'Ryan is 33 years old. He has been in Jamaica for seven years. Still, for him, New York is his life. He talks to his neighbors, his cousins, his mother, and his daughter, now eight, every day. He showed me his cell phone. All of the calls he had made recently were to New York. O'Ryan says he understands he made mistakes, but finds it difficult to see it as fair that he should pay the rest of his life for those mistakes. He does not see a future for himself in Jamaica, where he feels like a foreigner. O'Ryan was deported because he and his mother waited too long to apply for citizenship, and then there was an unexpected delay in his citizenship application. A bureaucratic mishap turned into a lifetime punishment for O'Ryan. Moreover, with access to legal counsel, O'Ryan may have been able to make the case that he was indeed a naturalized citizen and thus should not be deported. However, without these resources, he has been sent to Jamaica where he has to struggle to piece a life together.

Federica is another example of a legal permanent resident deported for an aggravated felony. In August 2001, ICE agents arrested Federica at her workplace and placed her in immigration detention. She was ordered deported on the basis of a 1996 criminal conviction. Moreover, her conviction was classified as an aggravated felony, meaning Federica never had a chance to explain to the judge that she had not been in any trouble in the years since her conviction, nor that she had four U.S. citizen children who would be left without a mother. None of these facts are admissible evidence in an aggravated felony hearing. Federica was deported to the Dominican Republic and has not seen her children since.

Federica's troubles with the law stemmed from her marriage to a U.S. citizen who turned out to be a drug addict. When her husband was arrested for robbery in 1996, she was arrested as well, as an accomplice. Federica was convicted and spent several months in jail. When she got out, she divorced her husband and regained custody of her children. Federica soon remarried and had two more children with her new husband. Federica was glad to have the chance to start over and greatly enjoyed her new job at a nursing home where she cared for senior citizens. She thought her past was behind her and did not know that she could be deported for her earlier conviction until ICE agents arrested her in her home.

Deportation Laws Can Be Retroactive

The 1996 laws were implemented retroactively. This provision is a violation of due process because a person experiences an additional punishment for a crime that did not exist when they were originally convicted. A person who is caught smoking marijuana in 1988 might be given a $50 ticket. If they are caught again with a small amount of marijuana in 1990, they could have to pay another fine. In 1990, these two marijuana charges would not have led to deportation for a legal permanent resident. In 1996, however, the law was changed, and now the person faces automatic deportation. This constitutes a new penalty for a crime that did not exist when the crime was originally committed.

Jay is a Dominican citizen who was deported under the retroactive provisions of IIRIRA. Jay's family migrated to Brooklyn in the 1960s. Jay did all of his schooling in Brooklyn where he made friends with his Puerto Rican and Dominican neighbors. Jay did not complete high school, but got his GED when he was 19. Jay arrived in the United States as a legal permanent resident when he was six, and thus qualified for citizenship when he was 11. But, his parents did not apply for him, and he never applied for himself. He told me he was not aware that he could be deported.

When Jay was growing up, his parents took him to the Dominican Republic regularly for vacation. But, as soon as he got old enough to say that he would not go, he stopped going. He saw that as their thing: they are Dominicans and liked to go back to the island. He did not really see the attraction. When Jay left school, he was able to get low-paying jobs. However, he was enticed by the quick money he saw his friends making in Brooklyn, selling drugs. In addition, he tried cocaine, and liked it. He decided to start selling drugs, in order to earn fast money. In 1980, Jay and his girlfriend had a son. Soon afterwards, he was arrested for possession of cocaine. He was released, and cooled off for a bit. However, the lure of the money and of cocaine proved to be too much for him, and, eventually, he was back selling.

In 1983, Jay was arrested with 125 grams of cocaine. He was convicted of possession with intent to sell, and was sentenced to five years in prison. While in prison, he married his girlfriend and began to take college courses. When he was released in 1987, Jay found a job in a sports shop, and soon became a manager. A couple of years later, Jay and his wife decided to relocate to Massachusetts, to start their lives over.

Jay found a job with Coca-Cola, and moved up quickly in the company. He still had trouble staying away from alcohol and drugs, and decided to go into rehab. While in rehab, Jay got to know a variety of community leaders. They recognized his ability to connect with youth and his passion for his community, and gave him a job at a community organization when he got out of rehab. Around the same time, Jay and his wife had their second son.

Things seemed to be going very well for Jay. He became the director of a local AIDS prevention organization, and volunteered counseling youth about drug abuse prevention. He had been clean for three years, and had found his passion. Jay loved doing community work, and was good at it. Since Jay had been released from prison in 1987, he had been on bail from the INS, pending his immigration hearing. According to the laws in 1987, he was eligible for a hearing where the judge would look at his case, and his family and community ties in the United States and the Dominican Republic. For Jay, it seemed good that his case was delayed for many years, as he was amassing lots of evidence of his rehabilitation and reincorporation into society. He continued to wait for his hearing, and was confident he would win his case. His wife and children were U.S. citizens. He was a community leader. He had no trouble with the law since his release. He was drug and alcohol free.

In 1996, a law was passed—IIRIRA—that limited the judicial review of certain deportation cases. Under this new law, the judge could not take any of these factors into account. Jay's crime—narcotics possession with intent to distribute—made him automatically deportable. In 1997, 10 years after his release from prison, Jay finally had his hearing, under the new laws. He was deported to the Dominican Republic, leaving his wife and two kids behind. Jay had moved from the Dominican Republic when he was six years old, and had few connections in the country.

Moreover, Jay lost his family. Once he was deported, he eventually separated from his life partner of 30 years, and was unable to watch his children grow up. Without his income, his wife struggled financially. She had to solicit help from the government to maintain the household. Without Jay's encouragement and support, his sons never went to college. Jay talked to them on the phone, but the long distance put strains on their relationship. Jay paid for his crimes and was in the process of paying his debt to society when he was removed from all he knew and loved. Twelve years later, Jay has overcome his losses. However, the losses to his family and to his community are less easy to assess.

Melvin is another person whose life was dramatically altered because of retroactive deportation laws. Melvin was born in 1968 in Guatemala City. When he was 18, he moved to the United States as a legal permanent resident. Melvin began to work in flooring, and eventually started his own business. Melvin's business became very successful and he was able to provide a good life for his wife and two children. Melvin married his U.S. citizen wife in 1998, and they had two children soon after. They had a large house, several cars, a successful business and took frequent vacations. Life was good for Melvin and his family.

In 2005, however, his past came to haunt him. Ten years earlier, in 1995, Melvin had trouble with the law—the one time in his life that he had trouble. Melvin was driving down the highway with a friend of his. They saw a man lying in the street, and Melvin backed up to see what had happened. The car behind him put on the high beams, and Melvin couldn't see where he was going. He rolled over the man he had seen laying in the highway. Melvin was scared, and took off. A bad decision, he admits. The next day, the police came to his house. He was charged with a hit and run and involuntary manslaughter. It turned out that the man was already deceased when Melvin rolled over him, and the involuntary manslaughter charge was dropped. For the hit and run, he was given a six-year sentence. He served one year, and the remaining five years were suspended.

Melvin figured his past was behind him. He had done his time and had not been in trouble with the law since. He got married, had two kids, and was running a successful business. He was a legal permanent resident of the United States, and never expected immigration agents to bother him. In June 2005, ICE agents came knocking on his door. They took Melvin into custody and told him he was to be deported to Guatemala. Although this crime did not render him deportable in 1995, it did in 2005, when he was arrested. Melvin could not believe his life was crashing down like this. Melvin and his wife spent $15,000 on lawyers, trying everything they could. It did not work, and Melvin was sent to Guatemala.

Once Melvin got settled in Guatemala, his wife and children moved to Guatemala City. They sold their house in the United States and figured that the $200,000 they had in assets would be enough to get started in Guatemala. Unfortunately, it turned out that the life changes put stress on their marriage. After about a year and a half, they decided to divorce, and Melvin's wife went back to the United States with the kids. In the United States, she works in a gas station and lives with her mother. Their children's lives have changed drastically as a result of Melvin's deportation.

IIRIRA and AEDPA, passed in 1996, vastly expanded the definition of deportable offenses, making conviction of a wide array of crimes grounds for deportation. In addition, these provisions were retroactive. Retroactivity goes against a fundamental notion of fairness—that people should know the potential consequences of a guilty plea before entering one. Melvin and Jay had no way of knowing that they would be automatically deported for their crimes, because, when the crimes were committed, they did not lead to automatic deportation. The laws changed after they committed their crimes, yet the retroactive provisions of the law meant that they faced deportation under the new laws.

Criminalizing Border Crossing

IIRIRA contained a provision which indicated that a person who is unlawfully present in the United States for more than one year will be declared inadmissible for 10 years. This law further stipulated that people who are in the country illegally for more than one year, leave, and then re-enter the United States illegally, without waiting the mandatory 10 years, are subject to a "permanent bar." In practical terms, this means that people who break immigration law by entering the country illegally twice will be barred permanently from living in the United States. This stipulation even applies to the spouses and parents of U.S. citizens.

For example, consider the case of Sergio, the husband of Melissa, a U.S. citizen. In the spring of 2008, I spoke with Melissa, a native-born U.S. citizen who faced a difficult choice. She had fallen in love with and married a Brazilian man, Sergio. Sergio had violated the terms of his visa by overstaying his tourist visa. This infraction alone would not have prevented Sergio from adjusting his status from tourist to legal permanent resident. However, it became a problem when Sergio re-entered the United States after overstaying, and without remaining outside of the country for the requisite time period. Sergio was not aware of the requirement that he remain outside of the country after overstaying his tourist visa, and thought all was well, especially because the border agents had allowed him to re-enter without advising him of this problem. Nevertheless, because of these violations of the INA, the DHS ordered Sergio to be deported when he applied for legalization. In addition, Sergio became permanently ineligible for admission to the United States based on his immigration violations and was deported.

Legal permanent residents can also be deported for immigration crimes—crimes which are not usually punishable in the criminal justice system, yet which can lead to the deportation of legally present people. Walter, a citizen of the Dominican Republic, is an example of a legal permanent resident deported for immigration fraud. Walter took a boat to Puerto Rico when he was 15 and attempted to enter the United States illegally. However, he was caught and deported. When he was 19, Walter decided to try to migrate again. This time he went through Mexico and made it to New York City. Two years later, Walter met and married a U.S. citizen and obtained legalization in 1998 through family reunification laws. He intended to make his life in the United States; he worked at JFK Airport to support his wife and their two children. In 2004, Walter was stopped by police officers for a traffic violation. When the officer checked Walter's immigration status, he discovered Walter had an immigration hold. It turns out that Walter had an order to appear at immigration court because immigration investigators had figured out that Walter had failed to mention on his application for legalization that he had been deported from Puerto Rico when he was 15. This accusation of immigration fraud resulted in Walter's residency being rescinded—six years after he was granted residency. Walter spent four years fighting his case, but in 2008 he lost and was deported to the Dominican Republic—as a criminal alien. His crime: immigration fraud. According to data provided by the U.S. Department of Homeland Security (2010), one out of six people deported on criminal grounds were deported for immigration crimes such as this.

Deported without a Lawyer

In criminal law enforcement, due process provisions require the appointment of legal counsel to defendants who cannot afford it. The Supreme Court has decided that appointing legal counsel is necessary to ensure a fair trial and the erroneous deprivation of liberty. In a similar vein, legal scholar Beth J. Werlin argues that immigrants facing deportation have a significant liberty interest at stake and that they risk the likelihood of an erroneous deprivation of liberty when they undergo deportation proceedings without legal representation. The INA is remarkably complex and it is difficult for an immigrant to assess on his or her own whether or not he or she qualifies for cancellation of removal—the legal term for relief from deportation. In addition, decisions by lower courts and the Supreme Court constantly change the definitions and provisions, making it nearly impossible for someone without legal expertise to represent fully their own legal interests (Werlin 2000). In my interviews with deportees, I often encountered deportees who had exhausted their savings and that of their relatives paying attorneys' fees. I also spoke with people who it seemed may have had a chance for relief from deportation had they retained a lawyer. Peter is one such example.

Peter, a Jamaican citizen who lived in the United States from the age of 20 until his deportation when he was 40, never thought he would be deported. He didn't have any trouble with the law. He didn't hang around criminal elements. He worked in landscaping, the restaurant business, a steel factory, and did house painting. In 1997, he ran into problems. He got into an argument with his girlfriend. She called the police and said he stole money and jewelry from her apartment. Peter says she had lent him some money and had asked him to clean her gold jewelry. The total value of the items was $1,800. When his court date came up, she didn't show up for court, but the state pressed charges. Peter was sentenced to 11 months in jail, of which he served nine.

Once he was released, he thought all of that was behind him. It took a while for him to get back on his feet, but, eventually, he was able to get painting jobs and was doing fairly well for himself. One evening in 2005, the Nashville police had a report of a robbery. Turns out Peter looked like the perpetrator, and the police picked him up. They quickly established that it was not him. Instead of letting him go, the police officer asked Peter if he was Jamaican. When Peter told him he was, the officer asked, "Do you mind if I call immigration?" Peter said he didn't mind. He was a legal permanent resident, and didn't think he had anything to hide.

The officer called immigration, and they said that Peter had had a Notice to Appear in immigration court, and had not gone. Peter had never received the Notice. It turns out that his 1997 charge had set off an immigration warning. Peter was taken to the county jail, where he waited three weeks for immigration agents to pick him up. From there, he was taken to a Corrections Corporation of America private immigration detention center in Memphis, where he stayed for six weeks, and then to Louisiana, where he spent three months. Overall, he spent seven months detained by immigration agents before he was deported to Jamaica.

I asked Peter if he was sure his sentence was only 11 months. He said he was sure. I told him that people can be deported for theft, but only when the sentence is one year or more. He said that maybe it was because of his failure to appear. I asked him if he had an immigration lawyer. He said he didn't; he couldn't afford one. Peter may have been wrongfully deported. In immigration proceedings, people don't have the same rights as in criminal proceedings. That's why he was held at the county jail for 21 days without seeing a judge. That's why he was never given a lawyer. Peter wasn't even given a trial. He was simply detained, given a deportation hearing, and then sent back to Jamaica, the country he had left nearly two decades before.

Back in Jamaica, Peter had nowhere to go. His whole family is in the United States. He hadn't kept in contact with school friends. When he left, his friends didn't have telephones, so he couldn't call them. Back in Jamaica, people in his neighborhood scorn him for never sending anything back when he lived in America. They look down on him because he was in America for so long and came back empty handed. Peter was a productive member of U.S. society. He is a skilled worker and was consistently employed. He had a car and a place to live. Back in Jamaica, he is on the verge of homelessness and unemployment. Everyone who cares about him is in the United States, where Peter is not allowed to return.

Phillip is another deportee who may have successfully fought his case had he been provided with a lawyer. Phillip, a Jamaican, traveled to the United States in 1994, when he was 21 years old, on a temporary visa. He subsequently met and married a U.S. citizen. Under the immigration laws in place at the time, his marriage meant that Phillip qualified for legalization. He and his wife applied for him to become a legal permanent resident. Phillip and his wife had their first child shortly afterwards, in 1998. Their second child was born a year later, and was born severely disabled. She was born unable to see or hear, is confined to a wheelchair, and eats only from a feeding tube.

Phillip and his wife moved from their home in Silver Spring, Maryland to Boston, to be closer to his mother-in-law. Phillip did not report his change of address to the INS, and his legal permanent residence was delayed. When Phillip went to check on his application, he was told he had to re-apply. He did. The second time, he had a court date in Boston. On the way there, he was pulled over by the police, and was late for his court appearance. He told me that he missed his court date. Unbeknownst to him, his application was denied and he was ordered deported in 2001.

Phillip was not aware of this deportation order, and kept on with his life in the United States. He opened up a small vegetarian restaurant and also worked as a musician. With the money he made from this, he was able to support his children. He had three more children, all girls. When I spoke with him, the youngest was two years old. While on a road trip in Louisiana, Phillip was pulled over because the car he was driving had paper plates from another state. When the officer heard his accent, he checked with Immigration to see what his status was. When the officer contacted immigration agents, he found out that Phillip had a deportation order, and took him into custody.

Phillip most likely qualified for relief from deportation, based on the facts that he had lived in the United States for 13 years, is married to a U.S. citizen, and has a daughter who is severely disabled. However, Phillip was taken to a detention facility in an isolated part of Louisiana where he had no way to plead his case. Phillip spoke with a lawyer in Massachusetts, who told Phillip that he needed $3,000 to take his case.

Phillip did not have the money to pay. Phillip never retained an immigration lawyer. After three months in immigration detention, he was on a plane back to Jamaica.

After being deported to Jamaica, he moved in with his mother in one of Kingston's infamous ghettos. When I met him, he had been in Jamaica for 11 months. He still found it hard to think about anything other than the United States—his family, his business, his life. In the United States, he ran a restaurant, and worked as a musician in the evenings. In Jamaica, he feels lost and is unable to find gainful employment. His wife had to close his restaurant in the United States when he was in detention, as she was unable to take on that responsibility. He feels useless in Jamaica, as if in a foreign country. Having spent the prime of his life in the United States, his banishment is devastating. He told me, "It's like I am dead."

Living without Papers

The cases I discuss above deal with legally present residents who face deportation because of criminal convictions. However, you do not have to commit a crime to be deported. People who overstay their temporary visas, are denied asylum, or who cross the border illegally also can be deported. Many people who face deportation once were in the United States legally, yet have lost their legal status due to a failed asylum claim or visa violation. Although these non-citizens no longer have the legal right to be in the United States, they often form strong ties to the United States and deportation can be devastating for them.

Many asylum seekers who waited years for their deportation hearings formed families and had children in the United States. For them, losing their asylum cases meant losing the lives they had built in the United States. Prior to 1996, asylum seekers were not usually detained. Instead, they were given hearings at which they could make their claims to asylum. In addition, they were given renewable work visas so that they could remain in the United States legally while waiting to find out if they had been granted asylum. Many times, these asylum cases dragged on for years, even decades. As the years went by, asylum seekers made lives for themselves in the United States. The lives they made for themselves, however, are not considered in their asylum hearings. What is taken into account is whether or not they have a well-founded fear of persecution in their home countries.

Vern's story provides one example of an asylum seeker who lived legally in the United States before eventually losing his case and facing deportation. Vern fled an abusive family situation in Guatemala when he was 10 years old. He set out alone for the United States, but ended up in Mexico, where he spent 10 years working at a wholesale market in Mexico City. In 1991, when he was 20 years old, Vern finally achieved his goal of traveling to the United States. Once in the United States, he applied for political asylum. The INS issued him a work permit while his case was being reviewed, and he began to work in a frozen-food processing plant in Ohio. He met a Honduran woman, Maria, also applying for political asylum, and they began to date. Years went by, and each year, they received work permits from the INS that allowed them to continue working, and to remain legally in the United States. Confident their cases eventually would be resolved, Vern and Maria married, and had their first child in 1996.

In 1998, Vern received a notice that he should leave the United States—his asylum application had been denied. Vern was devastated; he had established a life in Ohio, and had few ties to Guatemala. He decided to stay, hoping that his wife's application would be approved, and that she could apply for him to legalize his status. Vern thought he had a good chance of obtaining legalization, and decided that his best bet was to remain in the United States. Vern was counting on two things happening: 1) that he would not be among the less than 3 percent of undocumented migrants apprehended by immigration officials; and 2) that his wife's temporary legal status would eventually be made permanent and he too could obtain legalization. Vern and Maria had another child together and set down roots in Ohio. Vern rose up the ranks in the food-processing plant, eventually becoming supervisor. Maria also worked there, but she worked on the line, and earned less.

Vern and his family had a comfortable life, but Vern lived in fear that immigration agents would come for him. To avoid this, he did everything he could to stay out of trouble with the police—he never drank, avoided making traffic violations, and abided the laws at all times. He learned English, took his kids on outings every weekend, and tried to blend in as much as possible. Although Vern was undocumented, he lived as a "model citizen."

It wasn't enough. One Sunday morning, two immigration agents came to Vern's house and arrested him in front of his children—aged 12 and nine. The immigration agents were part of a Fugitive Operation Team that was designed to find "fugitive aliens"—people like Vern who had ignored their deportation orders. Vern was put into detention, and, eight days later, he was in Guatemala, the country he had left nearly three decades before.

From 1991, when Vern applied for asylum until 1998, when his application was denied, Vern was lawfully present in the United States. Vern's unlawful conduct consisted in his failure to leave once he was issued a removal order in 1998. More than a decade later, immigration agents apprehended Vern in his home and he was forcibly removed from the United States. Vern was not given the opportunity to explain to a judge that he had not abided by his deportation order because he had already formed a family in the United States, and that his family depended on him to meet their daily needs. He also was not given the chance to explain that he had worked at the same job for 16 years, that he had never had any trouble with the law, that his two children were U.S. citizens, or that his wife was very close to attaining legal status, which could ensure his own legal status.

After being arrested by immigration agents, Vern was not given a hearing; he was simply deported. Deportation is "regulatory, not punitive, so constitutional provisions for due process and other rights of criminals [are] not applied" (Warner 2005: 64). It seems excessive to deny any form of judicial review to a person such as Vern who had lived in the United States for more than two decades, has U.S. citizen children, and has few, if any, ties to any other country. To deny Vern judicial review of his deportation order was to ignore the notions of due process and constitutional protections that are so important to the United States. It also ignored his human right to form a family and to be with his family.

When asylum seekers are denied asylum, their children who have grown up in the United States often suffer the most. Katy came to the United States when she was two years old, and knew nothing about Guatemala when, at the age of 15, immigration agents ordered her and her family deported. This deportation order turned her life upside down. "My last Christmas in the United States, I couldn't even think of anything to ask for; I had everything," Katy told me, as she reminisced on her life in the United States. Katy lived with her parents and her sister in a spacious house in suburban Louisiana. Her parents moved to the United States when she was two years old, and were able to achieve the American dream. They had a house, several cars, and two daughters headed for success. Katy's father had his own business painting cars, her mother was a housewife, and Katy was a typical American teenager. On weekends, she went out with her friends to the mall or the movies. Tears streamed down her face when she thought of all she had lost—of the life she once lived.

Katy was finishing up middle school, and her sister was enrolled in college when they were deported from the United States. This was their worst nightmare. When the immigration agents arrived, they handcuffed Katy, who was waiting at the school bus stop. "It was in front of everybody," she told me. Katy's father and sister were taken to a county jail, and Katy and her mother were allowed to stay at a friend's house for their last four days in the country. Although Katy had been in the United States for 13 years, and her father had been in the United States since before she was born, they had not successfully legalized their status, and were deported to a country Katy knew nothing about.

When they were deported to Guatemala, Katy could not believe how drastically her life had changed. They were fortunate that they had a place to go—Katy's grandmother had passed away and left them a house. However, it was a simple dwelling, with adobe walls, a tin roof, and the bathroom was outside on the patio. It is already difficult to be an adolescent, and Katy did not deal well with this fall from riches to rags. She fell into a deep depression, and barely left the house for over a year. Unable to read or write Spanish, she never went back to school. In the United States, Katy excelled in school, was popular with her friends, and never got into trouble. She had dreams of becoming a veterinarian, and her sister was already studying to be a doctor. Upon deportation, their dreams were shattered.

People facing deportation are denied due process protections because deportation is not technically considered punishment. For people who have spent many years in the United States and have developed strong community and family ties to the United States, however, deportation is one of the worst imaginable punishments. For many deportees, deportation means being permanently separated from their spouses and children. When deportation is an additional consequence of a criminal conviction, when it involves permanent separation from loved ones, and when it shatters dreams, it is hard to see the logic in the claim that deportation is not punishment.

DISCUSSION QUESTIONS

1. What are some of the procedural protections denied to non-citizens facing deportation?
2. What does it mean to say that deportation is regulatory not punitive?
3. What are some of the provisions of the 1996 laws—IIRIRA and AEDPA?
4. On what basis could one claim that deportation is double jeopardy?
5. Use one of the case studies to explain how the absence of judicial review could affect a legal permanent resident's petition to remain in the United States.
6. How is the retroactive nature of the 1996 laws a violation of due process?

IV: Conclusion

~~~~~~

I n the United States, deportation is an administrative procedure and occurs without due process protections. This is particularly ironic in the United States because: 1) due process protections are at the heart of the U.S. Constitution and 2) the United States is a land of immigrants. Technically speaking, people facing deportation do not have due process protections because deportation is not punishment. And, people can be detained without a bond hearing or without being accused of a crime because detention is not prison. In this book, we have seen how people experience deportation as punishment and detention as prison. The question we now turn to is: Why does the United States deny due process protections to non-citizens? Why does an 1893 Supreme Court decision continue to hold today, in a very different world?

To answer this question, we must take seriously the idea of belonging, as deportation depends on a particular understanding of who belongs where. Citizenship implies territorial belonging, the right to live in your land of citizenship. If you lack citizenship in the United States, technically, you do not have the *right* to be in the United States; remaining within the United States is a *privilege* that can be revoked at any time. Deportation simply involves revoking that privilege. The idea that deportation is not punishment is based on a distinction between deportation and banishment, where banishment is punishment because it involves removing a person from a country where he or she belongs, yet deportation is simply returning a person to where he or she belongs, and thus is not punishment. This distinction was clarified in *Fong Yue Ting v. United States*, (1893), when the Court held:

> [deportation] is simply the ascertainment, by appropriate and lawful means, of the fact whether the conditions exist upon which Congress has enacted that an alien of this class may remain within the country. The order of deportation is not a punishment for crime. It is not a banishment, in the sense in which that word is often applied to the expulsion of a citizen from his country by way of punishment. It is but a method of enforcing the return to his own country of an alien who has not complied with the conditions ... which the Government of the nation ... has determined that his continuing to reside here shall depend. He has not, therefore, been deprived of life, liberty, or property without due process of law, and the provisions of the Constitution securing the right of trial by jury and prohibiting

unreasonable searches and seizures and cruel and unusual punishments have no application.

(*Fong Yue Ting v. United States* 1893)

According to this decision, which still holds in court today, deportation is an administrative procedure which ensures that people abide by the terms of their visas. When they do not, they face the possibility of being returned to where they belong. Remarkably, Justice Brewer's dissenting opinion from this 1893 case resonates today.

> [Deportation] deprives of "life, liberty, and property without due process of law." It imposes punishment without a trial, and punishment cruel and severe. It places the liberty of one individual subject to the unrestrained control of another. ... Deportation is punishment. It involves—first, an arrest, a deprival of liberty, and, second, a removal from home, from family, from business, from property. ... Everyone knows that to be forcibly taken away from home and family and friends and business and property, and sent across the ocean to a distant land, is punishment, and that oftentimes most severe and cruel. ... But punishment implies a trial: "No person shall be deprived of life, liberty, or property without due process of law." Due process requires that a man be heard before he is condemned, and both heard and condemned in the due and orderly procedure of a trial, as recognized by the common law from time immemorial.

The 1893 *Fong Yue Ting* decision continues to prevail today even though, when that decision was made, deportation looked very different. At that time, the statute of limitations on deportation meant that after a year in the United States people were no longer subject to deportation. In addition, there was no interior enforcement of immigration laws, meaning that deportation nearly always applied to people arriving in the United States, not to long-term residents (Kanstroom 2000). Today, however, the situation is quite distinct, with no statute of limitations on deportations, and the frequent removal of long-term residents of the United States.

The denial of due process to non-citizens in the United States rests on the false premise that immigrants are not part of U.S. society and that removing them simply involves returning them to where they belong. It is not difficult to see, however, that a non-citizen can develop significant ties to the United States and feel a sense of belonging in this country. More than one in ten persons in the United States is an immigrant (Immigration Policy Institute 2009). Even more people are the children and spouses of immigrants. Tearing immigrants from the fabric of our society is not an issue to be taken lightly. This sentiment was evident in the interviews I conducted with deportees: nearly all considered their deportation to be a penalty for infractions they committed in the United States. Many regretted not having the opportunity to contest their deportation orders in a court of law. Many thought their cases may have turned out differently had they had effective assistance of counsel.

Many deportees experience their deportation as banishment, and not as returning them to where they belong. Phillip, described above, told me that being deported made him feel as if he were dead. He was forcibly separated from all that gave his life meaning: his wife, his children, and his work. Moreover, this separation happened without due process. Phillip did not have the chance to explain to a judge why he should not be deported from the United States. As members of our society, don't long-term residents of the United States facing deportation deserve due process in their immigration hearings? Do they deserve bond hearings if they are to be detained? Do they deserve appointed counsel if they are to be tried? Do they deserve the opportunity to present equities in their favor if they are to be deported? Denying non-citizens these procedural protections makes a strong statement about citizenship and belonging. Deportation is not considered punishment because deportees do not belong in the United States.

The idea that certain people belong in the United States and others do not has a long and tarnished history. Citizenship defines official belonging to the national polity. From 1790, when the first U.S. citizenship law was passed, until 1868, when the 14th Amendment was incorporated into the Constitution, citizenship was for whites only. Prior to 1868, blacks had no citizenship rights in the United States. And, blacks who were enslaved had no family rights, as slave children were the property of their master and could be sold at his will. Today, nearly all people deported from the United States are non-whites. In fact, over 95 percent of deportees are from Latin America or the Caribbean. The current deportation regime repeats our history of exclusion, and reinforces exclusionary ideas about who belongs in the United States and who does not.

The *Fong Yue Ting* court decision also made it clear that immigration policy is not a domestic matter: it is a matter of national security and sovereignty and thus remains in the domain of the Executive and Legislative Branches. Immigration *is* a matter of national security when we think of who the United States allows to *enter* the country. And, in 1893, the *Fong Yue Ting* decision applied nearly exclusively at the border, as there was no interior enforcement of immigration laws. Yet, today, increasing numbers of immigrants are removed from their homes in the United States. In addition, deportation has become an extension of the criminal justice system, especially with the merging of criminal and immigration law enforcement we have seen in the aftermath of September 11, 2001. Thus we have a situation where we are relying on a doctrine based on national security to tear long-term residents of the United States from their homes, families, and communities. Moreover, deportation is becoming a collateral consequence of criminal convictions that is meted out only to non-citizens and without the due process protections provided in the criminal justice system. Deportation has begun to look more and more like punishment as it has increasingly become an additional consequence of a criminal conviction.

Today's court justices are increasingly realizing that deportation can have punitive consequences and have made decisions that bring some protections to people facing deportation. A prime example of this is the 2010 Supreme Court decision in the case of *Padilla v. Kentucky*. Deportation proceedings happen primarily in immigration courts, which are in the Executive Branch of the government. On occasion, immigration decisions are appealed and reach the Judicial Branch by way of the district courts and even the Supreme Court, as happened with the *Padilla* case. The *Padilla v. Kentucky* case revolved around whether or not the petitioner had received ineffective assistance of counsel as he was not advised of the deportation consequences of his guilty plea. The Court opined that:

> Although removal proceedings are civil in nature, deportation is nevertheless intimately related to the criminal process. Our law has enmeshed criminal convictions and the penalty of deportation for nearly a century. And, importantly, recent changes in our immigration law have made removal nearly an automatic result for a broad class of noncitizen offenders. Thus, we find it "most difficult" to divorce the penalty from the conviction in the deportation context. Moreover, we are quite confident that noncitizen defendants facing a risk of deportation for a particular offense find it even more difficult.
>
> (*Padilla v. Kentucky* 2010)

This Court decision—*Padilla v. Kentucky*—may mark the beginning of a new era. This decision specified that Padilla merited the right to effective counsel, given the grave consequences of deportation. It may be the case that the federal courts will be able to force more due process protections onto deportation proceedings. However, the implementation of due process protections for immigration proceedings would require a massive overhaul of the current system. Such a massive change would need to emerge from the Legislative Branch, not the Judicial Branch. The implementation of due process protections to immigration proceedings will require changing the laws.

A change in the laws that govern the removal of immigrants from the United States will require a national conversation on immigration. The United States claims to be a nation of immigrants, a nation of laws and justice, and a diverse society with equal protections for all. The denial of due process to immigrants constitutes a contradiction to these core values.

DISCUSSION QUESTIONS

1. What is the difference between banishment and deportation?
2. Which of the three court opinions presented in the Conclusion do you find most compelling? Why?
3. Is deportation punishment?
4. What is the relationship between citizenship and belonging?

Bibliography

Abandoned: The Betrayal of America's Immigrants. 2000. David Belle and Nicholas Wrathall, U.S., 55m (16mm, doc). Distributed by Bullfrog Films, PO Box 149, Oley, PA 19547.

Alderman, Ellen, and Caroline Kennedy. 1991. *In Our Defense: The Bill of Rights in Action.* New York: Harper Collins.

Amnesty International. 2008. "Jailed without Justice: Immigrant Detention in the United States." Retrieved May 2, 2011 (http://www.amnestyusa.org/uploads/JailedWithoutJustice.pdf).

Brennan Center. November 2006. "Citizens without Proof." Retrieved April 11, 2011 (http://www.brennancenter.org/page/-/d/download_file_39242.pdf).

Casas-Castrillon v. Lockyer. October 16, 2007. No. 07–56261 Florence Immigrant and Refugee Rights Project Amicus Brief. Retrieved October 4, 2011 (http://ccrjustice.org/files/CasasCastrillon_Amicus_07_10_17.pdf).

Cole, David. 2002. "In Aid of Removal: Due Process Limits on Immigration Detention." *Emory Law Journal 51*: 1003–39.

Coleman, Mathew. 2007. "Immigration Geopolitics Beyond the Mexico/US Border." *Antipode 39*(1): 54–76.

Danticat, Edwidge. 2007. *Brother, I'm Dying.* New York: Alfred A. Knopf.

Demore v. Kim. 2007. Supreme Court of the United States. Demore, District Director, San Francisco District of Immigration and Naturalization Service, et al. v. Kim No. 01—1491. Argued January 15, 2003. Decided April 29, 2003. Retrieved June 13, 2011 (http://www.law.cornell.edu/supct/html/01-1491.ZS.html).

Detention Watch Network. 2008. "About the U.S. Detention and Deportation System." Retrieved October 4, 2011 (http://www.immigrantjustice.org/sites/immigrantjustice.org/files/Detention%20Isolation%20Report%20FULL%20REPORT%202010%2009%2023.pdf).

Dow, Mark. 2004. *American Gulag.* Berkeley: University of California Press.

Fong Yue Ting v. United States, 149 U.S. 698 (1893). Retrieved June 12, 2010 (http://supreme.justia.com/us/149/698/case.html).

Fragomen, Austin. T. 1997. "The Illegal Immigration Reform and Immigrant Responsibility Act of 1996: An Overview." *International Migration Review 31*(2): 438–60.

Golash-Boza, Tanya. 2012. *Immigration Nation: Raids, Detentions and Deportations in Post 9/11 America.* Boulder, CO: Paradigm Publishers.

Grable, David. 1997–98. "Personhood under the Due Process Clause: A Constitutional Analysis of the Illegal Immigration Reform and Immigrant Responsibility Act of 1996." *Cornell Law Review 83*: 820–65.

Huffington Post. May 15, 2010. "Deportation Nightmare: Eduardo Caraballo, US Citizen Born in Puerto Rico, Detained as Illegal Immigrant." Retrieved April 11, 2011 (http://www.huffingtonpost.com/2010/05/25/deportation-nightmare-edu_n_588788.html).

Human Rights First. 2009. "U.S. Detention of Asylum Seekers: Seeking Protection, Finding Prison." Retrieved July 27, 2011 (http://www.humanrightsfirst.org/wp-content/uploads/pdf/090429-RP-hrf-asylum-detention-report.pdf).

Human Rights Watch. 2009. "Forced Apart (by the Numbers): Non-Citizens Deported Mostly for Non-Violent Offenses." Retrieved April 6, 2010 (www.hrw.org/node/82173).

Immigration Policy Institute. September 16, 2009. "Citizenship by the Numbers." Retrieved June 13, 2011 (http://www.immigrationpolicy.org/just-facts/citizenship-numbers).

INS v. Lopez-Mendoza, 468 U.S. 1032 (1984). Retrieved October 4, 2011 (http://supreme.justia.com/us/468/1032/case.html).

Inter-American Commission on Human Rights. Organization of American States. 2009. "Report on Immigration in the United States: Detention and Due Process." Retrieved April 28, 2011 (http://cidh.org/pdf%20files/ReportOnImmigrationInTheUnited%20States-DetentionAndDueProcess.pdf).

———. 2010. "Report No. 81/10." Publication. Case 12.562. Wayne Smith, Hugo Armendariz, et al. v. United States. Retrieved October 5, 2011 (http://cejil.org/sites/default/files/Final%20Report_CIDH_Wayne_Smith.pdf), n. 56 p. 55.

Kanstroom, Daniel. 2000. "Deportation, Social Control, and Punishment: Some Thoughts about Why Hard Laws Make Bad Cases." *Harvard Law Review 113*: 1890–1935.

Kerwin, Donald, and Serena Yi-Ying Lin. 2009. "Immigrant Detention: Can ICE Meet its Legal Imperatives and Case Management Responsibilities?" Migration Policy Institute. Retrieved August 1, 2011 (http://www.migrationpolicy.org/pubs/detentionreportSept1009.pdf).

Magna Carta online. Retrieved April 25, 2011 (http://www.constitution.org/sech/sech_044.txt retrieved April 25, 2011).

Markowitz, Peter. 2008. "Straddling the Civil-Criminal Divide: A Bifurcated Approach to Understanding the Nature of Immigration Removal Proceedings." *Harvard Civil Rights–Civil Liberties Law Review 43*: 289–351.

———. 2010. "Deportation is Different." *Working Paper No. 38*. Benjamin N. Cardozo School of Law. Retrieved October 4, 2011 (http://www.isholatarin.com/In-the-News/Deportation-is-Different.pdf).

Miguel-Miguel v. Gonzales. 2007. No. 05-15900. Appeal from the United States District Court for the District of Arizona. Argued and submitted July 13, 2007. Filed August 29, 2007. Retrieved October 4, 2011 (http://www.ca9.uscourts.gov/datastore/opinions/2007/08/29/0515900.pdf).

Morawetz, Nancy. 2000. "Understanding the Impact of the 1996 Deportation Laws and the Limited Scope of Proposed Reforms." *Harvard Law Review 113*(8): 1936–62.

National Immigrant Justice Center. September 2010. "Isolated in Detention." Retrieved October 4, 2011 (http://www.immigrantjustice.org/sites/immigrantjustice.org/files/Detention%20Isolation%20Report%20FULL%20REPORT%202010%2009%2023.pdf).

Office of Inspector General of the Department of Homeland Security. 2009. "Removals Involving Illegal Alien Parents of United States Citizen Children." Retrieved 12 November, 2010 (http://www.dhs.gov/xoig/assets/mgmtrpts/OIG_09-15_Jan09.pdf).

Padilla v. Kentucky. 2010. No. 08–651. Argued October 13, 2009. Decided March 31, 2010. Retrieved June 14, 2011 (http://www.supremecourt.gov/opinions/09pdf/08-651.pdf).

Patel, Sunita, and Tom Jawetz. 2007. "Conditions of Confinement in Immigration Detention Facilities." Briefing Materials. Retrieved October 10, 2008 (http://www.aclu.org/pdfs/prison/unsr_briefing_materials.pdf).

Pauw, Robert. 2000. "A New Look at Deportation as Punishment: Why at least Some of the Constitution's Criminal Procedure Protections Must Apply." *Administrative Law Review 52*: 305–45.

Salinas, Lupe. 2004. "Deportations, Removals, and the 1996 Immigration Acts: A Modern Look at the Ex Post Facto Clause." *Boston University International Law Journal 22*: 245–307.

Siskin, Allison, and Ruth Ellen Wasem. 2005. "CRS Report for Congress: Immigration Policy on Expedited Removal of Aliens." Congressional Research Service September 30. Retrieved October 4, 2011 (http://trac.syr.edu/immigration/library/P13.pdf).

Soeoth v. Keisler. October 29, 2007. No. 07-55549 American Civil Liberties Union Appellant Brief. Retrieved April 12, 2011 (http://www.aclu.org/files/pdfs/immigrants/soeoth_v_keisler_appelleesbrief_pt1.pdf and http://www.aclu.org/files/pdfs/immigrants/soeoth_v_keisler_appelleesbrief_part2.pdf).

Souter, Justice. 2003. Opinion of Souter. No. 01.1491: 538 in matter of *Demore v. Kim.* Retrieved April 15, 2011 (http://www.law.cornell.edu/supct/pdf/01-1491P.ZX).

Thangaraja v. Ashcroft. 2004. No. 02-73970 Memorandum. Disposition submitted July 30, 2004. Retrieved October 4, 2011 (http://archive.ca9.uscourts.gov/coa/memdispo.nsf/pdfview/082504/$File/02-73970.PDF).

Transnational Records Access Clearinghouse. 2006. "How Often is the Aggravated Felony Statute Used?" Retrieved October 5, 2011 (http://trac.syr.edu/immigration/reports/158).

United Nations Human Rights Council. 2008. *Promotion and Protection of All Human Rights, Civil, Political, Economic, Social and Cultural Rights, Including the Right to Development.* Report of the Special Rapporteur on the Human Rights of Migrants, Jorge Bustamante. Addendum Mission to the United States of America. March 5, 2008. Retrieved October 5, 2011 (http://texascivilrightsreview.org/tcrr/docfiles/un_rapport_2008/bustamante_2008_us.pdf), p. 8.

U.S. Department of Homeland Security. 2009. "Definition of Terms." Retrieved December 7, 2011 (http://www.dhs.gov/files/statistics/stdfdef.shtm).

U.S. Department of Homeland Security. 2010. Office of Immigration Statistics. Policy Directorate. "Immigration Enforcement Actions: 2009." Retrieved October 4, 2011 (http://www.dhs.gov/xlibrary/assets/statistics/publications/enforcement_ar_2009.pdf).

Vile, John R. 2006. *A Companion to the United States Constitution and its Amendments.* Westport, CT: Praeger.

Warner, Judith Ann. 2005. "The Social Construction of the Criminal Alien in Immigration Law, Enforcement Practice and Statistical Enumeration: Consequences for Immigrant Stereotyping." *Journal of Social and Ecological Boundaries 1*(2): 56–80.

Werlin, Beth J. 2000. "Renewing the Call: Immigrants' Right to Appointed Counsel in Deportation Proceedings." *Boston College Third World Law Journal 20*: 393–425.

Wessler, Seth Freed. 2011. "A Year after SB 1070, the Deportation Pipeline Still Begins in Washington." Colorlines Online. Published April 25, 2011. Retrieved October 4, 2011 (http://colorlines.com/archives/2011/04/a_year_after_sb_1070_the_deportation_pipeline_still_begins_in_washington.html).

Zadvydas v. Davis, 533 U.S. 2001. p. 690. Retrieved October 4, 2011 (http://supreme.justia.com/us/533/678/case.html).

Glossary/Index

A

administrative removal: the removal of an alien under a DHS order based on the determination that the individual has been convicted of an aggravated felony or certain other serious criminal offenses. The alien may be removed without a hearing before an immigration court. 3, 7

aggravated felony: a category of criminal offenses that includes any crime of violence or theft offense for which the term of imprisonment is at least one year, illicit drug offenses, as well as other violations 23, 24, 26

    deportation for 27, 29–31

Alderman, Ellen 2

American Convention on Human Rights (ACHR) 28

Amnesty International 19, 22

Anti-Drug Abuse Act 1988 23

Anti-Terrorism and Effective Death Penalty Act (AEDPA) 1996 26, 27, 34

appeal, right to 2, 7

appeals 21–22

    asylum seekers 20, 21

    long-term residents 16–19

    undocumented migrants 7

Armendariz, Hugo 28–29

asylum seekers/asylees: people who move across borders in search of protection from persecution 3

    alternatives to detention 22

    children of 40

    credible fear interview 19, 20

    deportation after losing cases 38–41

    detention of 3, 12, 19–21

    Joseph Dantica 10

    and separation of powers problem 21

B

banishment 24, 42, 44
bond hearings 15–16, 21
border crossing 6, 34–35
Border Patrol 5, 8, 19
Brandeis, Justice 25
Brennan Institute for Justice 14
Brewer, Justice 24–25, 43
burden of proof 4, 7, 13–15
Bureau of Immigration Appeals (BIA) 16, 18

C

cancellation of removal 7, 36
Caraballo, Eduardo 15
Casas-Castrillon v. Lockyer 2007 15
Ceballos, Armando Vergara 14–15
children
    of failed asylum seekers 40
    U.S. citizen 13, 23, 28, 29
citizenship 13–15, 30, 31, 32, 42, 44
    living without 8
Civil Rights Act 1964 27
Cole, David 11
Coleman, Matthew 6
constitutional protections 11, 24, 25, 26
    Fifth Amendment 11, 25, 26
    Fong Yue Ting v. United States 24–25, 42–43, 44
    not applicable to deportation proceedings 2, 6, 7, 8, 11, 24, 39–40, 42–43
criminal alien: a non-citizen who has committed a crime and is subject to deportation 4
criminal deportee: a non-citizen who has been convicted of a crime and subsequently deported 4–5

D

Dantica, Joseph 10
Demore v. Kim 2007 15, 16
Department of Homeland Security (DHS) 3, 11–12, 15, 16, 22
    deportation statistics 4, 8, 23
    detention of asylum seekers 3, 12, 20
    detention statistics 2–3
    streamlining process for immigration cases 8

deport: to remove an inadmissible or deportable alien from the United States based on an order of removal 1

deportable alien: an alien who has been admitted into the United States but who is subject to removal pursuant to provisions of the Immigration and Nationality Act (INA § 237) 3, 15–16

deportation
    see **removal**

derivative citizenship: citizenship conveyed to children through the naturalization of parents or, under certain circumstances, to foreign-born children adopted by U.S. citizen parents, provided certain conditions are met 13

detain: to seize and incarcerate a non-citizen in order to hold him or her while awaiting judicial or legal proceedings or return transportation to his or her country of citizenship 11, 13

detention: the place of incarceration of non-citizens awaiting judicial or legal proceedings or return transportation to his or her country of citizenship 2, 3
    see also **immigration detention**

discretionary power of judges, removal of 26, 27–31

Dow, Mark 3, 4

due process: the establishment of appropriate procedures prior to subjecting anyone to punishment or the deprivation of liberty 1, 2, 11
    1996 laws and denial of 26–35
    dissenting opinions on right to 16, 25
    and immigration law 5–8, 11
    move to protections for immigration proceedings 45
    not applicable to deportation 2, 5, 6, 7, 8, 11, 39–40, 42–43
    protection in criminal justice system 5, 7, 35
    and undocumented migrants 7

E

entry
    illegal re- 8, 27
    seeking 6

Ex Post Facto Clause 24

Executive Office for Immigration Review (EOIR): an agency of the Department of Justice that administers the nation's immigration court system 21

expedited removal: when an immigration officer orders a person deported without any further hearing or review. This requires a finding that the alien is inadmissible. 3, 5, 6–7, 19

F

Fifth Amendment 11, 25, 26

Fong Yue Ting v. United States 1893 24–25, 42–43, 44
formal removal 7
Fourth Amendment 24
Fragomen, Austin 3, 5

G
Golash-Boza, Tanya 3, 23
Grable, David 7

H
habeas corpus 11
Human Rights First 20, 21
Human Rights Watch 4, 20

I
illegal alien
    see **undocumented migrant/illegal alien**
Illegal Immigration Reform and Immigrant Responsibility Act 1996 (IIRIRA) 3,
    26, 33, 34
illegal re-entry, criminalization of 8, 27
Immigration and Customs Enforcement (ICE) 10, 13, 14, 15, 18, 21
    statistics 3, 4, 8
Immigration and Nationality Act (INA): the statutory basis of U.S. immigration
    law 3, 5, 23, 26, 35
immigration courts 21–22, 45
immigration crimes 34–35, 36–37
Immigration and Naturalization Service (INS) 3
immigration detention: a complex of Department of Homeland Security (DHS)
    detention centers, county and city jails, and privately owned prisons used to hold
    people awaiting immigration trials or deportations 2–4, 10–22
    alternatives to 22
    of asylum seekers 3, 12, 19–21
    average stay in 19
    and burden of proof regarding citizenship 13–15
    experiences of 12–13
    of legal permanent residents 16–19
    as preventative not punitive 11
    and right to bond hearings 15–16
    and separation of powers issue 21–22
    violation of due process and habeas corpus 11
    without a criminal record 18–19

immigration enforcement terms 3

immigration judge: an attorney appointed by the Attorney General to act as an administrative judge within the Executive Office for Immigration Review. They are qualified to conduct specified classes of proceedings, including removal proceedings. 4, 7, 21–22, 26
    removal of discretionary powers of 26, 27–31

Immigration Policy Institute 8, 43

inadmissible alien: an alien seeking admission at a **port of entry** who does not meet the criteria in the INA for admission. The alien may be placed in removal proceedings or, under certain circumstances, allowed to withdraw his or her application for admission. 3, 5, 6

INS v. Lopez-Mendoza 1984 5

Inter-American Commission on Human Rights 21, 28, 29

International Covenant of Civil and Political Rights (ICCPR) 28

J

Jawetz, Tom 11

judicial review: the power of the court to determine whether or not a law or administrative order is constitutional 7, 11, 22, 24, 26, 40

K

Kanstroom, Daniel 5, 7, 23, 43

Kennedy, Caroline 2

Kerwin, Donald 20

L

lawyer, access to a 35–38

legal permanent residents: foreign nationals who have been granted the right to reside permanently in the United States. Also known as green card holders. 1, 3, 4, 5, 8
    aggravated felony provisions and deportation of 27, 29–31
    deportation after criminal convictions 5, 14, 16–19, 25–26
    deportation for immigration crimes 35, 36–37
    detention without a criminal record 18–19
    retroactive deportation of 32–34

M

Magna Carta 2

mandatory deportation: deportation without judicial review 1, 23, 27, 28–29

mandatory detention 5, 15, 21, 23

Markowitz, Peter 5, 7, 24

Miguel-Miguel, Diego 18
Miguel-Miguel v. Gonzales 2007 18
Morawetz, Nancy 30

N
naturalization: the conferring, by any means, of citizenship upon a person after birth 14–15
Ng Fung Ho v. White 1919 25

P
Padilla v. Kentucky 2010 45
parolee: a foreign national, appearing to be inadmissible to the inspecting officer, allowed into the United States for urgent humanitarian reasons or when that alien's entry is determined to be for significant public benefit. Parole does not constitute a formal admission to the United States and confers temporary status only, requiring parolees to leave when the conditions supporting their parole cease to exist. 4, 20, 21
Patel, Sunita 11
Pauw, Robert 24
port of entry: any location in the United States or its territories that is designated as a point of entry for aliens and U.S. citizens. All district and files control offices are also considered ports, since they become locations of entry for aliens adjusting to immigrant status.
punishment 23, 24, 31
    Brewer's dissenting opinion on deportation as 42–43
    changing views on deportation as 45
    deportation feeling like 24–26, 40–41, 44
    deportation not considered as 26, 27

R
refugee: a person fleeing persecution who has been granted protection in another country 4, 19
Rehnquist, Chief Justice 15–16
removal: the compulsory and confirmed movement of an inadmissible or deportable alien out of the United States based on an order of removal 2, 4–5, 7, 23–41
    after a loss of legal status 38–41
    constitutional safeguards not applicable to 2, 6, 7, 8, 11, 24, 40, 42–43
    and denial of due process 26–35
    feeling like punishment 24–26, 40–41, 44
    for immigration crimes 34–35, 36–37
    of legal permanent residents with criminal convictions 5, 14, 16–19, 25–26

move to providing some protections for people facing 45
statistics on 4, 8, 23
types of 3, 6–7
violation of international treaties on handling of 28–29
without legal representation 35–38
retroactive clauses 7, 26–27, 31–34

S
Salinas, Lupe 25, 27
separation of powers issue 21–22
Sixth Amendment 26
Smith, Wayne 28–29
Soeoth, Raymond 20–21
Soeoth v. Keisler 2007 21
Souter, Justice 16

T
Thangaraja, Saluja 20
Thangaraja v. Ashcroft 2004 20
Transnational Records Access Clearinghouse 4
treaties, international 28–29

U
undocumented migrant/illegal alien: a person without proper documentation to be in the United States 4, 7, 8, 39
United Nations Human Rights Council 23
Universal Declaration of Human Rights 20

V
Velasquez, Joe 1, 2
Vile, John 2
voluntary departure: the departure of an alien from the United States without an order of removal. The departure may or may not have been preceded by a hearing before an immigration judge. 5

W
Warner, Judith Ann 40–41
Werlin, Beth J. 35, 36
Wessler, Seth 5
withdrawal: an arriving alien's voluntary retraction of an application for admission to the United States in lieu of a removal 3, 5

Y
Yi-Ying Lin, Serena 20

Z
Zadvydas v. Davis 2001 11